2nd Edition

INVISIBLE SCARS

HOW TO TREAT *COMBAT STRESS* AND *PTSD* WITHOUT MEDICATION

BART P. BILLINGS, Ph.D.

DocUmeant *Publishing*
244 5th Avenue
Suite G-200
NY, NY 10001
646-233-4366
www.DocUmeantPublishing.com

Invisible Scars

How to Treat Combat Stress and PTSD without Medication

Published by
DocUmeant Publishing
244 5th Avenue, Suite G-200
NY, NY 10001
Phone: 646-233-4366

Author's website: www.bartpbillings.com

Interior book and cover design by Let's Write Books, Inc.
Printed in the United States of America
2nd Edition Printing

Library of Congress Control Number: 2017949990
ISBN: 978-1-9378-0185-4

PRAISE FOR INVISIBLE SCARS

"Dr. Billings, if we had read your book about the dangers of many of the drugs that the VA gave our son, Corporal Andrew R. White, USMC to treat his PTSD I am positive that he would be alive today. His mother and I trusted the doctors who treated Andrew ...this was a big mistake. The cocktail of antidepressants (Paxil), antipsychotics (Seroquel®) and analgesic drugs killed my son. Since his death we have been on a mission to help other veterans obtain drug-free treatments for PTSD."
–Stan and Shirley White (Marine Corps parents) Davis, WV

"Dr. Bart Billings is alone in the ranks of military mental health in denouncing the pseudoscience of biological psychiatry with its invented 'disorders'/'diseases'/'chemical imbalances' and one-dimensional drugging/poisoning which damages the brain and body of every soldier & veteran while killing untold thousands—horrifically—by sudden cardiac death. This must end to make room for humane, non-medical therapies."
–Fred A. Baughman Jr., MD, board-certified neurologist

"*War causes fragmentation and destabilization of the combat warrior as it destabilizes the society in which it is fought. The art of physical medicine is utilizing physical remedies rather than medications to heal the WHOLE being—mind, body, and spirit. Hence the antidote for combat stress—a 'holistic' approach to healing.*"

–Chrisanne Gordon, MD, board-certified physiatrist, American Academy of Physical Medicine and Rehabilitation, founder and executive director, Resurrecting Lives Foundation

"*The enthrall and embrace of magic has captured our 21st century society. Nowhere is that better exemplified than in the field of psychopharmacology. As much as we may wish for an elixir that could magically heal mental health disorders, there is none. Dr. Billings has done yeoman service by underscoring that reality, as well as grim dangers that present when we rely on psychoactive drugs as a curative. We owe him a thank you!*"

–General David Brahms, Esq. (Ret. USMC)

"*The FDA, military services, and VA want to help patients, and certainly wish to deter suicide and violence. The problem is their one-size fits all commitment to antidepressants results in denying to patients the full truth. As the mental health expert and soldier that he is, Dr. Bart Billings' 'Invisible Scars'—utilizing integrative treatment modalities instead of psychiatric medication—is a must-read for those seeking the truth on military suicides, mass shootings, and what the media won't cover in these tragedies.*"

–Commander Don Farber, Esq., (Ret. USN,) .

"My late husband, William Glasser, MD would be so happy to see Bart Billings' book today. I believe he would say that it could quite possibly revolutionize the treatment of countless soldiers suffering from combat stress for all time. This book is a must-read by anyone who is seriously concerned about the tragic suicide rate among our service men and women returning from combat."

–Carleen Glasser, senior faculty The
William Glasser Institute International, author
and widow of the late William Glasser, MD

"Dr. Bart P. Billings brings more than three decades of military experience to this compelling expose of the dishonor shown the military and veterans who dodge bullets, grenades and explosives to safeguard their nation only to face—and often die from—dangerous psychiatric drugs prescribed them both on the battle field and at home. With veterans killing themselves at the rate of 22 a day, 'Invisible Scars' is an urgent wake-up call about the lethal dangers of chemically-overwhelming our military members and vets. It exposes how the psychiatric-pharmaceutical profiteers of multi-billion dollar military-psychiatric research, drugs and damaging brain-intervention methods offer not help, but betrayal.

–Bruce Wiseman, U.S. president of the Citizens
Commission on Human Rights, author

"Dr. Billings' book is insightful in describing the residual physical and mental effects of combat stress on our veterans. As a cardiologist, I see the relationship between stress and heart disease on a daily basis. Integrative medicine interventions are very effective in reducing levels of stress without the adverse effects of many pharmaceuticals."

–Mimi Guarneri, MD, FACC, president,
Academy of Integrative Health and Medicine
and author of The Heart Speaks.

TABLE OF CONTENTS

FOREWORD

This book may scare you, it may anger you, but it will certainly will educate you and help you learn how to work with people, both veterans and the general civilian population, who are suffering with normal reactions to very extreme negative situations in life.

Author Dr. Bart Billings has served in the U.S. Army for approximately thirty-four years, both as an enlisted combat engineer and a medical service corps officer. He has treated and educated tens of thousands of veterans as a clinical psychologist in the military and civilian private practice. He was the chief of professional services and the assistant director at the UC Davis Medical Center's Department of Physical Medicine & Rehabilitation, was the commanding officer for a U.S. Army Reserve general hospital section, has served on the Palomar College Heroes Education Board and has served on the California Governor's Advisory Board at Patton State Hospital.

He is a licensed clinical psychologist, holds a license as a marriage and family therapist, and is the director and founder (started it while in the military twenty-two years ago) of the longest running, now civilian, combat stress conference on the planet (International Military and Civilian Combat Stress Conference). He has appeared on numerous TV and radio news programs, and despite a successful career spanning nearly forty-eight years, where most others would welcome retirement, he has chosen to begin an especially sacrilegious path of exposing problems within his own field of mental health by writing this incredible book.

Dr. Billings' book acknowledges that veterans suffering with combat stress, just a few years ago, were committing suicide at the rate of twenty-two veterans per day; however, he now exposes in this book what many have noticed and seen in their clinical practices for the past several years—that people's normal reactions to extreme negative situations (aka "symptoms"), are becoming more chronic and difficult to treat because of the treatments being used.

Dr. Billings convinced the chairman of the Congressional Veterans' Affairs Committee of the U.S. Congress to hold hearings on Feb. 24th, 2010, and stunned the congressman with his and others' expertise and data showing that veterans were getting worse and even committing suicide *because of them using psychiatric medications!* Dr. Billings has studied, wrote, and lectured upon psychiatric medication induced suicide for decades and indicated, "I had to expose this because it is the right thing to do." His steadfast dedication to the spirit of humanity comes through clear and precise in this book as he clearly exposes how psychiatry and pharmaceutical companies have placed profit over people. Dr. Billings' work and book has won him celebrity status within the critical mental health community and in 2014, he received the International Human Rights Award from the largest and most effective nonprofit mental health watchdog group in the world, Citizens Commission on Human Rights International.

This is *the* only book specifically addressing and outlining how individuals experiencing combat stress are suffering longer and with worsening symptoms because of the massive use of psychiatric medications. Dr. Billings provides an uncensored description and data showing the dangers involved in taking psychiatric medications, and he explains in clear and concise terms how to work with individuals without the use of psychiatric medications.

This book is a must-read for anyone working in mental health and social work and those working with combat stress and what many call post-traumatic stress disorder (PTSD). Dr. Billings has a gold standard program, and this book is extremely relevant and needed at this critical time because literally hundreds of thousands of people are being given anti-psychotic medications, anti-depressant medications and anti-anxiety medications at epidemic rates, and with little to no evidence to support off-label usage.

With statistical analysis and compassion, Dr. Billings is able to demonstrate the United States is sitting on its own mental health chemical time bomb, whereby veterans, their families, and the general civilian population are being lost, murdered, incarcerated, and forgotten due to the use of psychiatric medications.

Toby T. Watson, Psy.D.

Clinical director and psychologist - Associated Psychological Health Services

Board member and past executive director - International Society for Ethical Psychology and Psychiatry

Former chief psychologist - State of WI Department of Corrections - KMCI

INTRODUCTION

The allure of "magical" solutions attracts many people in today's modern society, and nowhere is this fascination with magic better exemplified than in the field of psychopharmacology. Unfortunately, as much as we may wish for an elixir that could magically heal mental health conditions and disorders, there is none. Dr. Bart Billings' book has done yeoman service by underscoring that reality. His litany of grim dangers that present when we see such conditions and disorders should serve as a clarion call to end this practice. His strong and informed voice in these regards warrants a thank you!

I have known Dr. Billings for over twelve years in various capacities. I have known him as a clinical psychologist who is a retired military Medical Corps officer. He was the founder and director of the International Military and Civilian Combat Stress Conference, which was held for its first fifteen years at Camp Pendleton Marine Corps Base. This conference provided a seminal setting for exchanging ideas and sharing information regarding combat stress and the conditions spawned by it. I first met him in connection with that conference—first, as an attendee and later, as a presenter.

In his capacity as a clinical psychologist, I have had the opportunity to consult with him regarding Marine clients caught up in the military justice system. In some of those cases, I referred clients to him for psychological evaluations that assisted me to effectively represent those Marines. His insights were uncanny and extremely helpful in achieving positive results for my clients. I also consult with Dr. Billings on various situations involving Marines and their families, as well as veterans I assist under the aegis of various non-profit entities. I have seen first-hand his concern for the well-being of veterans and their families. Such has always been one of his top priorities. Indeed, that was the impetus for him to write this book.

I have been a Marine for fifty-two years (twenty-five of which was in active duty service). I have an intimate understanding of the problems Marines and their families' encounter both in times of war, as well as peace. In my practice I regularly have to wrestle with the perplexing issues presented by active duty service members and veterans suffering with post-traumatic stress and the destructive impact of the drugs used to treat them.

By happenstance, I discovered Dr. Billings' combat stress conference. It quickly filled my need. Attendance as a participant led to my being a presenter. These experiences were seminal.

In my view, Dr. Billings' focus on integrative treatment for military persons and veterans is right on target. His strong opposition to utilizing mind-altering psychiatric medication as the course of choice is well grounded. His warnings regarding the dangers inherent in using such drugs are a public service of the first order. Kudos is in order.

General David Brahms, Esq. (Ret. USMC)

DEDICATION

Colonel Jimmy Brusitus, MS, (Ret. Army)

Jimmy was one of the most important people in my life, and in the memory to his service to our country, he is one of the individuals I want to dedicate this book to. Jimmy was a military hero in Vietnam, a professor at West Point, and as a civilian, helped with the resurrection of Bosnia after their war. We attended college together and he was the best man at our wedding and my first daughter's godfather. Before he died, he spoke at our combat stress conference on two separate occasions, giving firsthand knowledge on the topic of combat stress.

William Glasser, MD

The late Dr. Bill Glasser was instrumental in providing me with my professional foundation on how to be an effective therapist. His strong influence on all aspects of my life, from raising my children to working with patients, has had a lasting influence on my life decisions. He taught me the value of providing therapy without the use of psychiatric medications. His reality therapy/choice theory psychology approach was applicable not only for mental health treatment, but for management, educational, and community service work.

General Richard Lynch, DO, (Ret. Army)

Dr. Richard Lynch gave me the opportunity to be "All You Can Be" in the Army. Not only was he my commanding officer for many years, but also to this day remains a very supportive close friend. He saw the value of teaching people how to deal with combat stress' residual effects on our soldiers and made arrangements for me to present the programs I developed with my colleagues to the policy and planning generals at the Pentagon.

Jean Marie Billing, my wife of forty-seven years

Jean Marie, has helped me in so many ways and continues to support my work and passion. From volunteering, along with my daughters, Julieann and Tiffany, at the initial combat stress conferences to helping to register attendees as well as performing extensive administrative work, she has always been there. It is tradition in the military that when an Army officer is promoted, a spouse gets an insignia one rank higher. She wears her one star, deservedly so after my thirty-four years of service, with honor on occasion.

CHAPTER 1

MENTAL HEALTH TREATMENT PROGRAMS IN THE UNITED STATES

Since the mid-1970s I have argued, contrary to the established belief of the American Psychiatric Association (APA), that post-traumatic stress (PTS) is a normal reaction to an abnormal experience. In one of my first psychology courses in undergraduate school we had to read *Man's Search for Meaning*, which was written by an icon in the field of psychology/psychiatry, Dr. Viktor Frankl. As a survivor of four Nazi concentration camps during WWII, he was very familiar with the stresses of war. In his book, he states what I have been stating in my teachings for the last forty years: "An abnormal response to an abnormal situation is normal behavior."[1] In the case of our military personnel, the trauma and stress being experienced is a normal psychological and physiological re-

---

1   Frankl, V. (2006). *Man's search for meaning*. Boston: Beacon Press.

sponse to combat conditions. It only becomes a disorder (PTSD) if the person is unable to figure out (with or without professional help) how to reconnect with their idea of normal. Without normalization, the symptoms cause a continual disruption of their lives. For example, as a nineteen-year-old college student, I experienced a tragic event that today would, more likely than not, qualify me as having post-traumatic stress (PTS). Driving home late one night, the car in front of me was broadsided by another car traveling at a high rate of speed. I immediately stopped and attempted to assist the victims. Both passengers had been violently ejected through the front windshield and were lying approximately thirty feet from their car. As an Eagle and Explorer Scout, I had a rudimentary understanding of first aid, which I hoped would be helpful. I immediately became aware that the elderly couple's injuries were severe and beyond my abilities; I was unable to even recognize any distinct facial features. They had died instantly, which was confirmed by the paramedics at the scene.

Given the severity of the injuries I witnessed, this extraordinarily traumatic experience stayed with me for a significant period of time. The trauma was very much a part of my thoughts, and I absolutely was experiencing post-traumatic stress from that very abnormal situation. For a few nights I had nightmares about the accident, and since I drove that same route quite often, I was always anxious and hypervigilant when approaching the intersection. However, I was able to work through this traumatic event by completing my college work, working a part-time job, and leaning on my extended family and close friends by discussing what I had experienced. By taking advantage of my routine—school, job, family, and friends—I was able to get back to my normal. This does not mean, however, that I will ever forget that harrowing event.

Even today, when driving through the intersection where the accident happened, I still have visions of what occurred that evening. This experience did not affect my life to the point where I was unable to continue toward my goals and live a happy and productive life. Simply continuing to meet my psychological needs in a healthy and productive manner circumvented any long-term trauma and stress that could have been associated with this traumatic event. In short, I experienced a *normal* reaction to an *abnormal* situation and, because of the many interactions integrated into my daily activities, I was able to get back to normal. This daily integration, or what later I recognized as an integrative wellness treatment program, does work.

What doesn't work when treating PTSD is the widespread use of brain-altering psychiatric medications. Over the years I've observed a direct correlation between the increased use of psychiatric medications to treat PTSD and TBI (traumatic brain injuries) and the high rate of military and civilian suicides and other abnormal and/or violent behavior.

On the other hand, as you will see in later chapters, integrative treatment programs that do not utilize psychiatric medications are not associated with increased suicides and violent behavior.

To illustrate the relationship between psychiatric medication and adverse psychological effects, one needs only to look at the black box warning on these psychiatric medications.

WHAT IS A BLACK BOX WARNING?

A black box warning is the warning that alerts a user of a prescription medication that he or she may experience serious side effects from the drug. The name derives from the typical black border surrounding the warning.

The FDA states that a "black box warning means that medical studies indicate that the drug carries a significant risk of serious or even life-threatening adverse effects. The U.S. Food and Drug Administration (FDA) can require a pharmaceutical company to place a black box warning on the labeling of a prescription drug, or in literature describing it. It is the strongest warning that the FDA requires."[2]

These warnings alert doctors and pharmacists to serious complications associated with the given medication. For example, most antidepressant and antipsychotic medications are required to have black box warnings that describe their side effects and risks, as well as emphasize the need for close monitoring of patients starting on these medications. The FDA has also determined that "a Patient Medication Guide (MedGuide) should be given to patients receiving

---

2   Black Box Warning. (n.d.). Retrieved November 14, 2015, from https://blackboxwarning.wordpress.com/

these drugs to advise them of the risks and subsequent precautions that can be taken."[3]

RECENT EXPERT WITNESS EXPERIENCE

I recently was enlisted as an expert witness in a court case involving an Air Force veteran who was suing the Veterans Administration for what he believed was inappropriate and damaging mental health treatment. Arizona attorney Larry Berlin was aware of my decades-long work with PTSD within the military/veteran population and had heard about the International Military and Civilian Combat Stress Conference I founded and have continued to direct for the past two decades. Berlin wanted my expertise in this case and was confident I would be able to help his client win his lawsuit.

Berlin provided me with volumes of medical records from the VA, depositions, and other mental health program records. I also asked that the veteran come to San Diego so I could conduct a proper evaluation. After reviewing the medical records and spending most of the day carrying out a complete psychological exam with the veteran, I was shocked by not only what I had read in his medical records but also by what the veteran revealed to me during the evaluation. The veteran had spent twenty years in the U.S. Air Force logging thousands of hours

---

3   FDA Launches a Multi-Pronged Strategy to Strengthen Safeguards for Children Treated With Antidepressant Medications. (2004, October 15). Retrieved November 14, 2015, from http://www.fda.gov/NewsEvents/Newsroom/PressAnnouncements/2004/ucm108363.htm

in electronic surveillance aircraft. The veteran enjoyed his Air Force career and had even obtained a Master's degree, becoming fluent in both Hebrew and Korean during his service. Upon his retirement from the Air Force, the veteran had been accepted into a doctoral program and was teaching at two community colleges. He was married, had a family, and owned his own home. Remarkably, he was training for a private pilot's license and it's fair to say that at that point in his life, his future was bright and filled with optimism. This well-disciplined military veteran followed retirement protocol by reporting, with medical records in hand, to the nearest VA hospital. During his initial evaluation, the veteran explained that his only significant medical problem was gastrointestinal. While in the military, the veteran had no history of any mental health issues.

The veteran's initial evaluation resulted in a diagnosis of PTSD. This diagnosis was rendered based on the veteran's discussion of experiencing gastrointestinal (GI) problems. As a result of the PTSD diagnosis, the veteran was prescribed an antidepressant. Within a brief period of time, the veteran developed a Parkinsonian-type tremor, which, on occasion, is consistent with the medication he was given. The psychiatric medication he was given listed, as a side effect, this type of tremor. The adverse drug event was never dealt with appropriately and, as is typical in psychiatric treatment, the answer was to increase the dose and try other psychiatric drugs.

As a result of the failure of the treating physician to consider possible medication related causes of the tremor, the veteran left the VA with increased amounts and various types of psychiatric medications for years to come. This was the beginning of the veteran's downward spiral into a world altered by multiple prescribed psychiatric medications. As a result of being so heavily medicated, the veteran was unable to maintain his employment at the community colleges, dropped out of the doctorate program, and eventually divorced.

The veteran would continue his treatment with the VA for nearly fifteen years. The high doses of medication caused the veteran to lose his ability to walk; for nearly eight years, he was relegated to a wheelchair for his mobility. It wasn't until a new physician at the VA raised the possibility that the veteran's inability to ambulate was due to the cocktail of psychiatric drugs that the veteran actively pursued another course of treatment.

The veteran took his doctor's opinion seriously and requested to participate in a VA-sponsored inpatient detoxification program. When the VA refused, he sought out a private program with a price tag of more than $30,000. The veteran entered the private program in his wheelchair and, in less than twenty days of detoxifying from the psychiatric medications, was able to walk out of this program with only a minor Parkinsonian-type tremor in one arm, which was the result of years of brain-altering medication. The initial damage to the veteran's physiology took time to heal, but eventually he recovered physically and returned to a healthy, psychiatric-drug free life style. This veteran's case, like so many others, was the result of a simple misdiagnosis; it was tragic and could have been avoided.

During his military career, this veteran had spent thousands of hours in aircraft that produced high intensity/low-frequency vibrations, and one of the symptoms of Vibroacoustic disease is gastrointestinal difficulty. Other symptoms can include pericardium thickening, vascular lesions, certain types of cancer, anger, and hostility. The veteran had reported to the VA physician that he had gastrointestinal difficulties and also had a lesion on one of his legs. The physician conducting the initial evaluation failed to consider the possibility of Vibroacoustic disease. Instead of being referred to a GI specialist, he was treated as someone suffering from mental health issues. I feel strongly that if the veteran had been referred to a GI specialist at the initial evaluation, he would have been spared the devastation to his health and his life would be totally different today.

A judge in federal court heard the case at the end of 2014 and the outcome of this trial resulted in the Plaintiff appealing to the Ninth Circuit Court of Appeals from the District Court's ruling denying liability. Over a fourteen-year period, the VA gave the plaintiff approximately 450 prescriptions consisting of almost 25,000 psychotropic pills, many of which caused devastating adverse side effects and none of which were actually needed. The lower court did not find any deviation from the standard of care of treatment. The Plaintiff and his attorney are hopeful and optimistic that the Ninth Circuit Court of Appeals will reverse the lower court's decision.

While this case may be surprising to most people, it is not uncommon for a veteran to be misdiagnosed and wrongly prescribed psychiatric medications with significant adverse side effects, including those with a black box warning for suicidality.

In 2002, I spoke with a U.S. Navy occupational medicine physician at the International Military and Civilian Combat Stress Conference. He was confused as to the numerous accidents that sailors experienced—such as walking off the deck or walking in front of aircraft—especially when there seemed to be no logical explanation for these accidents. At that point in time, I had been studying Vibroacoustic disease (VAD). This syndrome is caused by High Intensity/Low Frequency (HI/LF) sound, which results in physical and psychological damage. Sometimes, this condition goes unreported, and other times it is mistakenly diagnosed as PTSD.

Knowing how serious this condition could be, the physician requested that I write an article for the Navy's Medical Journal on the subject. The comprehensive article I eventually wrote for Navy Medicine, titled "Feeling the Sound Can Be Dangerous to Your Health," described the effects and possible dangers of long-term exposure to excessive levels of HI/LF sound—sounds commonly produced by battlefield noise, airplanes, machinery, highly amplified bass music, and race cars. Not only can these sounds be physically harmful, but they can also cause potentially fatal complications.

I believe that it is critical for mental health professionals and general medicine practitioners to be aware of VAD so that a misdiagnosis of PTSD can be avoided. This service member's sad story is a clear illustration of someone who was suffering from VAD but was given a diagnosis of PTSD and was prescribed psychiatric medications for 15 years.

The example below is from a relatively recent Pennsylvania lawsuit brought by a veteran against the VA. The lawsuit alleges that the veteran received inappropriate mental health treatment at the VA Hospital, where excessive amounts of brain-altering medications were prescribed.[4]

---

4   Laskowski et al v. Department of Veteran Affairs, No. 3:2010cv00600 - Document 112 (M.D. Pa. 2011). Retrieved November 25, 2015, from https://casetext.com/case/laskowski-v-us-dept-of-veteran-affairs.

IN THE UNITED STATES DISTRICT COURT FOR THE MIDDLE DISTRICT OF PENNSYLVANIA

Stanley P III and Marisol Laskowski VS United States Of America / Department Of Veteran Affairs,

Before – The Honorable James Munley

Place – Courtroom No.3

Proceedings – Non-jury trial

Date – Tuesday, September 18, 2012

Appearances – For Plaintiff; Daniel Brier, Esq. and John Dempsey, Esq. – For the Defendant; George Michael Thiel, Esq.

Marine Sergeant Laskowski successfully sued the VA (receiving in excess of three million dollars) for the inappropriate standards of mental health care. The trial revealed that the discharged Marine Sergeant Laskowski was given excessive amounts of brain-altering psychiatric medication.

The excerpt (below) from the trial transcript shows how the attorney for the Department of Justice (DOJ) tried to sway the judge's decision to deny the Marine justice. The DOJ attorney (Attorney Thiel), representing the government, stated in open court:

"Your honor, but that's exactly the message that's going to be sent. Open the flood gates because a verdict in favor of the plaintiff, that's how it's going to read."

The response to the DOJ attorney's implication of opening the floodgates, which was given by the plaintiff's attorney (Attorney Brier) was very powerful. His response to the implication that if Judge James M Munley rules in favor of the plaintiff, that the flood gates will be open for future lawsuits of this nature. (Located on page 58, line 6 through line 14 of the same court transcript.).

Attorney Brier said, " Judge, how dare they? How dare they come here and try to intimidate you about opening the floodgates? I'll tell you what you should do; Judge, put it on the front page of the New York Times that when you serve this country and don't get the health care you are entitled to, a judge will hold the biggest government accountable. How dare they for saying, 'Okay, Judge, you will open the floodgates, we screw a lot of these people up? How dare they?'"[5]

The actions of the attorney for the government in this Pennsylvania trial relates to the aforementioned trial in Arizona, where Attorney Berlin was representing a veteran. This sentiment by a DOJ attorney may be something to ponder when considering the negative outcome for Berlin's client in the previously mentioned Arizona trial.

To further help you understand the harmful effects of brain-altering psychiatric medication I would like to make reference to Dr. Peter Breggin, who wrote *Medication Madness*, which is about the inappropriate and often harmful prescriptions asso-

---

5   Laskowski et al v. Department of Veteran Affairs, No. 3:2010cv00600 - Document 112 (M.D. Pa. 2011). Retrieved November 25, 2015, from https://casetext.com/case/laskowski-v-us-dept-of-veteran-affairs.

ciated with psychiatric medication. In Chapter 1 of *Medication Madness,* Dr. Breggin describes an individual who went to his family physician complaining of a back problem and left the doctor's office with a prescription for an antidepressant. Within a very short period of time, this person considered killing himself and his wife. There was no prior history of mental health or family problems. Dr. Breggin described the overwhelming desire the man felt to take his life, even making an attempt to obtain a firearm by driving his car into a police officer and physically trying to take the officer's handgun when he was on the ground. The individual was subdued by the police officer and a bystander and jailed. He later was released from jail with a diagnosis of toxic effects from medication(s) with no further charges filed in this case.

Another example of an adverse reaction to brain-altering psychiatric medication was former heavyweight champion Chris Byrd, whom I met when he was speaking at a sports wellness workshop. Based on the information he shared with me about his experience with psychiatric drugs, I asked Chris to join me on a radio sports talk show in San Diego where I had been scheduled to discuss adverse effects of psychiatric medications. Chris explained on the radio show that he never had any history of mental health or family problems. He had been experiencing a physical problem that had resulted in inflammation of his foot. Although he had various evaluations to determine the cause of the inflammation, no significant findings were determined. Rather, his physician prescribed, off-label, an antidepressant to reduce his foot pain. Soon after taking the prescribed psychiatric drug, Chris began to contemplate suicide and, on occasion, was experiencing inexplicable outbursts of anger. Since psychiatric medications mask unusual behavior from the person taking them, Chris did not realize his inappropriate behavior. Fortunately for Chris, his wife believed there might be a connection between his very unusual behavior and the antidepressant that he was taking. When the level of concern reached the point of Chris' teenage son having to stay home from school to watch his father due to Chris' suicidal ideation, his wife immediately requested that he stop taking the antidepressant.

Chris stated that he was weaned off the medication and very quickly returned to normal without any further thoughts of suicide or inappropriate outbursts of anger. It should be noted, however, that Chris' adverse reaction to the psychiatric medication he was prescribed was consistent with the black box warning on the medication. Alternative reasons for Chris' inappropriate behavior and suicidal ideation, as well as why he may have been more susceptible to adverse drug reactions, is explored in Chapter 4.

The article "Psychiatric Drugs Create Violence and Suicide" is part of a psychotropic drug series that was recently published by the mental health human rights group The Citizens Commission on Human Rights International (CCHR). The report states, "It is not unusual for people to misunderstand the difference between psychiatric disorders and medical diseases." CCHR describes how conditions are "only labeled a disease after it has met strict standards; you have to isolate a predictable group of symptoms, be able to locate the cause of the symptoms and see how they function. This must all be proven and established by a physical test such as a blood test or x-rays. In psychiatry, there are no lab tests to identify disorders."[6]

Consistent with the above CCHR article is the statement by Dr. Darshak Sanghavi of Harvard Medical School, who disagrees with the "chemical imbalance" theory: "Despite pseudoscientific terms like 'chemical imbalance,' nobody really knows what causes mental illness. There's no blood test or brain scan for major depression. No geneticist can diagnose schizophrenia."[7] He's not alone: "The World Psychiatric Association and the U.S. National Institute of Mental Health even admit that psychiatrists do not know the causes or cures for any mental disorder or what their 'treatments' (usually drugs) specifically do to the patient."[8]

Stephen Sharfstein, former president of the American Psychiatric Association, admitted, "There is no clean-cut lab test to determine a chemical imbalance in the brain."[9]

While seeing hundreds of patients over the many years I have been in the mental health field, it's quite obvious to me that when individuals experience emotional difficulties, it is generally a reaction to stresses experienced in life. At times their reactions to life problems can become incapacitating. But to imply that these difficulties are medical diseases caused by a chemical brain imbalance is misleading. Treating these situational reactions to life circumstances with psychiatric medications has the potential

---

6   Antianxiety drugs: The facts about the effects. (n.d.). Retrieved October 25, 2015, from http://www.cchr.org/sites/default/files/education/anti-anxiety-booklet.pdf
7   Psychiatric drugs create violence and suicide. (n.d.). Retrieved October 25, 2015, from http://www.cchr.org/sites/default/files/education/violence-and-suicide-booklet.pdf
8   Mood Stabilizers: The Facts About the Effects. (n.d.). Retrieved October 25, 2015, from http://www.cchr.org/sites/default/files/education/mood-stabilizers-booklet.pdf
9   (2005, July 11). *People*.

to lead to harmful adverse reactions that can destroy ones individuality and at times can even be deadly.

It bears repeating: "What psychiatric drugs do instead is mask the real cause of problems, often denying you the opportunity to search for workable, effective solutions … [and therefore] allowing yourself to be treated with psychiatric drugs is very risky, since there is very little science to back it up."[10] Be aware that for psychiatrists and pharmaceutical companies to sell any psychiatric drugs, they must come up with a marketing campaign, stating that a chemical imbalance in the brain causes mental disorders and that drugs correct that imbalance. This marketing hype is repeated on television, radio, movies, and in the printed media so often that millions of people around the world are led to believe this as fact. Not only do psychiatrists and (at times) family physicians misdiagnose our veterans, it also is becoming the rule, rather than the exception, for anyone experiencing normal reactions to traumatic life situations be diagnosed with a mental disorder and given psychiatric medication(s). Even off-label psychiatric medication prescriptions, as mentioned in the above case (Chris Byrd), is not uncommon.

If you want to research the topic further, the book written by Peter C Gotzsche, MD, titled *Deadly Psychiatry and Organized Denial* gives an in-depth look at what has been discussed in the previous paragraphs. Dr. Gotzsche is an internal medicine physician with advanced degrees in chemistry and biology, and he has also worked in the drug industry for eight years.

---

10 Antidepressants: The Facts About the Effects. (n.d.). Retrieved October 25, 2015, from http://www.cchr.org/sites/default/files/education/anti-depressants-booklet.pdf

TAKING EFFECTIVE CONTROL OF YOUR LIFE

During WWII, combat stress was not called battle disease or battle disorder, but rather battle fatigue. When anyone is fatigued, the best way to overcome it is through rest and relaxation, or R&R. This was the most common way to treat battle fatigue during World War II. When soldiers were too mentally and/or physically fatigued to be effective on the battlefield, they were most often sent to the rear areas for R&R. After continuous fighting, it was not unusual for whole units to be relieved and sent to the rear for R&R.

Since battle fatigue was not considered a disease or disorder, soldiers were not generally given mind-altering psychiatric medications. With a sufficient amount of time for R&R, soldiers were able to return to combat. When their time in the military was completed, they were able to return to the civilian world without a psychiatric label identifying them as damaged goods. Today when our soldiers come back from combat, they often return with a label stating that they have a disease or disorder from being in combat.

The amount of time for R&R allotted to our current soldiers to reintegrate into the civilian world is basically nonexistent; it's not even close to the amount of time soldiers from World War II were given. Many WWII soldiers, when completing their time on the battlefield, experienced weeks, if not months, of non-combat assignments and R&R before they returned home.

Veterans who develop actual physical injuries, upon discharge, deserve immediate treatment and disability benefits from the VA. Problems that are the result of combat vary from soldier to soldier. Exposure to Agent Orange and other toxic substances can later bring about significant physical problems such as cancer and Parkinson's. Also TBI, and chronic traumatic encephalopathy (similar to NFL football players, whose life expectancy is much lower than the average general population), can show up years later and interfere dramatically with the veteran's life. In these cases, it is undeniable that soldiers should be treated immediately and compensated appropriately, not only for the physical problems, but also for the accompanying emotional problems.

Also included in veteran's health services and benefits should be all people diagnosed with long-term PTSD, since along with the well-known emotional problems, many can develop physical problems such as heart disease and diabetes. This occurs as a result of not dealing effectively with the initial PTS, which can lead to long durations of flight-or-fight autonomic neurological arousal. But with implementation of appropriate longer-term transitional programs, PTS should never be allowed to turn into PTSD, as has been the case for over a decade. This is truly a preventable problem and can be most-readily handled by implementing transitional programs (which I'll elaborate on in Chapter 11).

INSIGHTS DEVELOPED DURING THE PAST TWENTY-TWO YEARS AT THE COMBAT STRESS CONFERENCE

Over the years of directing the International Military and Civilian Combat Stress Conference, attendees with multiple deployments have stated that they personally have seen an increase in psychiatric medication on the battlefield and they have observed various abnormal behaviors with individuals on psychiatric medication, including suicide. Since 2005, a surge in psychiatric medication prescriptions in the military, as well as in the civilian population, coincides with the gradual increase in suicides. Through my substantial work with active duty military personnel and veterans, I have concluded that there is a direct relationship between psychiatric medications and suicide/homicide.

Military and VA psychiatrists most often prescribe these psychiatric medications, even though they result in an increased risk for suicide. In reviewing the data regarding those who commit suicide, as well as homicide, the majority of these people (even if they never had a history of mental problems) were taking some type of psychiatric medication. And these psychiatric medications carry the previously mentioned black box warning that cautions for suicidality and a host of other adverse reactions, including abnormal behavior, mania, psychosis, poor judgment/reasoning, anger, and hostility, which can translate to homicide and depression.

Brain-altering drugs will most definitely change a person's behavior simply by virtue of the fact that they significantly alter the naturally occurring chemicals in the brain. The question is whether the drug is actually treating a confirmable abnormality.

When I was preparing for the fifteenth annual combat stress conference at Camp Pendleton, I had an opportunity to speak with the base's commanding general. We got into a discussion about then a recent newspaper article in the San Diego Union Tribune by Rick Rogers that reported on the wide disbursement of psychiatric medications to Marines on the battlefield. When I asked him what he thought of this recent policy, his response was surprising. He stated that if a Marine has an infection, he receives medication for that disease; if a Marine has a mental health disease, he saw no reason why he/she should not receive medication for that disease. I explained, in detail, that an infection is a very measurable physical problem that can be observed through X-rays and blood work; the medication, consisting of an antibiotic, would cure the infection with minimal, if any, side effects. On the other hand, someone labeled as having PTSD has no scientific tests, conclusive blood work, or X-ray that can identify it as a disease. The symptoms are a normal reaction to being in combat. I explained that symptoms or behaviors only become PTSD when they interfere with one's functioning, and if this is the case, the Marine should not be deployed.

My observations have been that psychiatric medications do not cure anything, but rather blunt a person's senses; soldiers taking them often state that they feel like zombies. These psychiatric medications have black box warnings that indicate residual effects, including suicide, poor judgment and reasoning, anger, and hostility. In the past, soldiers were not allowed to be deployed to combat if they were on any type of psychiatric medication. When I asked the general if he would take any of the psychiatric medications that his troops were deployed with, he strongly stated he would never take psychiatric medications. The conversation ended when I asked him how he could sanction his Marines being given psychiatric medications when he would not personally take them himself.

All psychiatric diagnosing is subjective and based on the opinion of the treating physician/psychiatrist. But the danger of violent behavior and suicidal ideation is compounded for combat veterans who may also have suffered traumatic brain injuries (TBI), a medically verifiable injury to the brain.

TRAUMATIC BRAIN INJURIES (TBIS)

A TBI can be detected by a brain scan where there is noticeable tissue damage, along with observable physical impairment, i.e. range of motion difficulties and coordination problems. When a person has suffered a TBI, the injury itself increases the likelihood of committing suicide by approximately four times, compared to those who have never been exposed to a TBI or CTE. Compounding the problem is the fact that those suffering from TBI, more likely than not, are referred to psychiatrists because of the TBI or CTE symptoms such as anxiety, depression, forgetfulness, and frustration.

A psychiatrist is not a specialist in brain injuries. The simple fact is that unlike neurologists or physiatrists, psychiatrists do not extensively study physical injuries or diseases of the brain and, therefore, have little or no place in the diagnosis or treatment of those suffering from a brain injury. There is no place for a psychiatrist's prescription pad in the treatment of brain injuries. Primarily neurologists and physiatrists (physical medicine and rehabilitation, or PM&R, doctors) are trained to work with this population. Unfortunately, in most cases, a psychiatrist winds up giving the patient psychiatric medications, which do not treat the actual brain injury. Since the 1970s, a large majority of psychiatrists have prescribed brain-altering medications to most of their patients. It is well accepted within the psychiatric community that prescribing psychiatric drugs is a typical form of psychiatric treatment.

According to a New York Times article by Gardiner Harris entitled "Talk Therapy Doesn't Pay, So Psychiatry Turns Instead to Drug Therapy," psychiatrists generally no longer provide talk therapy as a form of mental health treatment. A psychiatrist, in most instances, is prescribing patients that have the potential to kill themselves medication that carries the black box warning for suicidality. If a person with a history of TBI is four times as likely to commit suicide, it would be reasonable to expect that if this person was prescribed a dangerous psychiatric medication, then the suicide risk would increase exponentially.[11]

---

11   Harris, G. (2011, March 5). Talk Doesn't Pay, So Psychiatry Turns Instead to Drug Therapy. Retrieved October 25, 2015, from http://www.nytimes.com/2011/03/06/health/policy/06doctors.html?pagewanted=all&_r=0

A serious mental health problem is exemplified when one looks at the Department of Defense (DoD) drug purchasing between 2005 and 2011. "There was approximately a 700% increase in purchasing psychiatric medications."[12] The result of this action is dramatically revealed in the following figures. According to figures released by the DoD in 2013, "479 members of the military - 259 active duty personnel, 87 reservists, and 133 members of the National Guard - committed suicide."[13] The simple truth is that there is an epidemic of suicides among veterans and, based on data collected by the VA, "it is estimated that 22 veterans killed themselves each day."[14] My 2010 congressional testimony in Chapter 6 gets into specific details on increased psychiatric medications and increased risks of suicide.

In 2012, after researching suicides among military/veterans, Assistant Secretary of Defense Jonathan Woodson, MD sent a letter to members of the U.S. Army Medical Command (MEDCOM) directing them to reduce the levels of antipsychotic medication they were prescribing for PTSD. That was a positive step, but as far as I know or have seen, Woodson failed to follow up, taking no action on the over-prescribing of antidepressants. However, since psychiatrists were more than likely involved in Woodson's research, there seems little

---

12   Friedman, R. (2013, April 6). Wars on Drugs. Retrieved October 25, 2015, from http://www.nytimes.com/2013/04/07/opinion/sunday/wars-on-drugs.html
13   Kime, P. (2014, July 22). Military suicides declined slightly in 2013, Pentagon says. Retrieved October 25, 2015, from http://archive.navytimes.com/article/20140722/NEWS05/307220072/Military-suicides-declined-slightly-2013-Pentagon-says
14   Wing, N. (2013, January 14). Military Suicides Reached Record High In 2012. Retrieved October 25, 2015, from http://www.huffingtonpost.com/2013/01/14/military-suicides-2012_n_2472895.html

doubt about why the prescribing of antidepressants remained allowable. "The greatest concern," wrote Dr. Woodson, "is the suspicion of the over-prescription of antipsychotic medications for PTSD." Woodson's statement included Seroquel®, (often referred to as Serokill by military personnel) a powerful anti-psychotic that was being prescribed off-label to soldiers for sleep disorders and irritability associated with PTSD.[15] One of the positive results from Dr. Woodson's report was increased awareness that integrative treatment should be elevated in status when providing treatment to our veterans. In other words, there are alternatives to medicating behavior.

According to a 2011 study by the VA published in the Journal of the American Medical Association, some patients received the antipsychotic drug Risperidone. However, the study revealed that this drug "was no more effective in treating PTSD than a placebo."[16] In fact, many of these veterans who took these drugs found that not only did the drugs not work, but that their emotions and relationships deteriorated.[17]

In a questionnaire that I was told about by an Army social worker at the annual combat stress conference I direct, veterans were asked why they did not want to report their PTS during military evaluations. Although I haven't seen the original questionnaire, according to the social worker, the number one reason

15   Friedman, R. (2013, April 6). Wars on Drugs. Retrieved October 25, 2015, from http://www.nytimes.com/2013/04/07/opinion/sunday/wars-on-drugs.html
16   Krystal, J., Rosenheck, R., Cramer, J., Vessicchio, J., Jones, K., Vertrees, J., . . . Stock, C. (2011, August 3). Result Filters. Retrieved October 25, 2015, from http://www.ncbi.nlm.nih.gov/pubmed/21813427
17   Krystal, J., Rosenheck, R., Cramer, J., Vessicchio, J., Jones, K., Vertrees, J., . . . Stock, C. (2011, August 3). Result Filters. Retrieved October 25, 2015, from http://www.ncbi.nlm.nih.gov/pubmed/21813427

vets did not want to discuss their PTS was that they did not want to be medicated. Their negative opinion of psychiatric medications is consistent with what they experienced, either when given meds or when observing their peers who were using these medications. Veterans that I have seen for therapy are much more receptive to talk therapy and are more cooperative in seeking mental health treatment when medication is not involved and integrative wellness is the treatment modality.

Dr. Evan Mayo-Wilson, an assistant scientist in the department of epidemiology at John Hopkins Bloomsburg School of Public Health, commented on *Bottom Line Health* that "Cognitive Behavioral Therapy (CBT) was more effective than antidepressants and other drugs in treating social anxiety disorder," and his assertion is based on more than two decades of research.[18] Along with other problems veterans may be experiencing, social anxiety is a behavior that often plagues returning veterans; it most often exhibits as fear and avoidance of interacting with others when returning from combat. This study is just one example of why talk therapy is more effective than psychiatric medications; over the past few years, there have been many news articles discussing inappropriate mental health treatment at various Veterans Administration Hospitals.

The reason talk therapy is effective in helping with social anxiety stems from the actual involvement with the therapist. The need for involvement with other human beings is a very

---

18   Mayo-Wilson, E. (n.d.). Better Treatment For Social Anxiety | Bottom Line Health. Retrieved October 25, 2015, from http://bottomlinehealth.com/heardbyoureditors/better-treatment-for-social-anxiety/

powerful higher-level need that most all human beings strive for. In talk therapy, the person providing the therapy establishes involvement and caring. This leads to trust between the client and the therapist, which can be learned by the client and applied to other social situations. Brain-altering medications given in 10 minutes by a psychiatrist do not help a person meet the need for involvement; the drugs teach the client nothing. They may even reduce the client's ability to become involved with others. (This will be discussed in detail in Chapter 9).

ATTEMPTS AT PUBLIC EDUCATION REGARDING APPROPRIATE MENTAL HEALTH SERVICES

In 2014, I appeared on various television shows, including the HBO news show *Vice* (Episode 10, "No Man Left Behind"), a few documentaries, and numerous national and international radio broadcasts. In all instances, I explained the dangers of psychiatric medication and the value of integrative treatment. The HBO show featured two veterans who were experiencing difficulties with psychiatric medications, including thoughts of suicide. By the time the show aired, one of the veterans had committed suicide. The show should have received national attention, especially since it clearly documented the difficulties veterans are having in receiving appropriate treatment. It also documented the suicide the veteran had been contemplating while filming the news story. During each of these media occasions, I made it clear that in my forty-eight years in the mental health field, I never once recommended to a mental health team the prescribing of psychiatric medication. Rather, I prefer, and utilize, integrative therapy because I can personally document from my experience, and others, that this alternative approach is more effective than prescribing brain-altering medications.

The 2014 and 2015 International Military and Civilian Combat Stress Conference was, for the first time in its history, actually held at a wellness center (Tri-City Wellness Center in Carlsbad, California). Tri-City has worked with veterans from nearby Camp Pendleton who are suffering from various combat injuries and associated emotional issues with significant success. The conference has, for more than two decades, allowed open discussion from active military and civilian personnel as well as reserve and retired veterans and their families on the emotional/behavioral changes experienced by individuals deployed to combat, family relationships, medical treatment, physical injuries, and effective treatment modalities.

As an educational forum, the conference is intended to encourage in-depth discussion by stakeholders in the mental health arena—not only in the United States but also throughout the world. And, over the years, there has been a gradual shifting toward integrative treatment as the choice for combat stress related problems. Integrative treatment programs or, as I prefer to call them, integrative wellness programs, take an in-depth look at an individual's physical and psychological needs and determine what combination of treatment modalities would improve his/her life situation.

In an integrative treatment program, each participant is provided with an individual wellness program (IWP) that is unique to his or her needs. There is no psychiatric medication involved with an IWP since there is no desire and, more importantly, need, to introduce a brain-altering substance that actually interferes with the overall wellness program outcome. Based on an individual's needs, the program may consist of a combination of counseling, nutrition, exercise, sporting activities, yoga, individual and group talk therapy.

Ultimately, the anticipated outcome of all wellness programs is to return the individual to being a normal, functioning member of the community. This is best illustrated by a wheelchair-bound basketball-playing veteran who explained it very clearly when he said, "Playing basketball is getting me back to normal." This veteran was a very active basketball player before he lost his legs and now, with the help of a sports wheelchair, he is doing what was normal to him before his injury. Bottom line was that this vet was looking at what he could do with what he had, instead of looking at what he could not do with what he did not have.

Another integrative rehabilitation success story occurred with a patient I worked with in a physical medicine and rehabilitation program at the University of California in 1979. I received a referral from the burn ward stating that there was a bilateral amputation patient who was severely burned. I went to see this patient and discovered that she had many significant mental health problems that had resulted in her current injuries. The patient had been a substance abuser, lost her children, never drove a car, and had no familial ties. Now she was severely depressed and in a hospital with a total sense of complete failure—even at trying to kill herself.

The twenty-eight year old woman was completely covered in bandages with only a slit for her to see. The backstory was that the patient had checked into a hotel room to commit suicide by overdosing on drugs. She passed out while smoking a cigarette, the bed caught fire, and her legs were so badly burned that amputation of both was necessary; she suffered burns on 90 percent of her body. During the patient's three-month recovery in the hospital, complete physical medicine and rehabilitation services were provided, including Reality Therapy/Choice Theory psychology. No psychiatric medications were prescribed, and as her physical wounds healed, the patient was gradually tapered off the pain medications. The patient received prosthetic limbs, learned how to drive, got her driver's license, enrolled in a community college program, reconnected with her family, and was making arrangements for her children to be returned. The patient was drug-free and her mind was clear for the first time in many years. This patient is a huge success. It's always amazing when a patient leaves the hospital with a significant impairment that they have learned to overcome and can say, "I'm better off now than I have ever been in my life."

The above experience, and others, greatly influenced my belief in integrative treatment, which can be seen as an outgrowth of physical medicine and rehabilitation. The success that has come from integrative treatment reinforces the need for its continued utilization within the veteran/military and civilian community. There are various types of integrative treatment modalities, including basic counseling, group therapy, spiritual counseling, nutrition, vocational counseling/training, hydrotherapy, biofeedback, guided imagery, equestrian therapy, yoga, acupuncture, and more. All of these treatment modalities are proven to be effective in getting people successfully functioning in the community at a fraction of the cost of long-term psychiatric medication and minus the possible serious side effects associated with them. Based on the success of those who have participated in this integrative wellness treatment, it is clear that physical medicine and rehabilitation, integrative medicine, and integrative wellness programs are the most effective treatments available for patients experiencing emotional/behavioral problems and facing enormous challenges.

CHAPTER 2

RECONCILING THE EFFECTS AND TREATMENT OF COMBAT STRESS NOW AND THROUGHOUT HISTORY

General George Patton, Jr., one of WWII's most famous generals, was known to be a military historian. He studied past military commanders and their battles dating back to the Greeks and Romans. Although Patton was a great leader when it came to military battles, his sentiments did not apply favorably to combat stress. While psychiatrists were advancing in their understanding of war trauma, the diagnosis of combat exhaustion was not universally accepted by military brass. Patton, like many other generals of the time, was notable in his lack of empathy for the psychological difficulties experienced by his troops. It is well known that Patton slapped two soldiers who were recuperating in a military hospital, yelling at a medical officer to not admit the soldiers to the hospital and to return them to the battlefield

President Roosevelt received thousands of letters about the incident, and ultimately Patton was reprimanded and ordered by the supreme allied commander, General Dwight Eisenhower, to apologize, relieved of command of the Seventh Army, and, as a result, was not allowed to participate in the D-Day landing in France. Combat stress reactions have existed from the beginning of time, and the trauma and stress related to the horrors of war have been referred to by many names more appropriate than "yellow bastard."

A "lack of moral fiber" or the "soldier's heart" (Civil War), "shell shock" (WWI), "combat neurosis," or "battle fatigue" (WWII), and "operational exhaustion" (Korea), are all labels associated with the psychological ravages of war. The most recent label, post-traumatic stress (PTS), is simply the latest term used to describe a normal reaction to abnormal events. PTS is not exclusive to military personnel; it also describes the symptoms civilians experience after observing, or being directly involved in, a traumatic event.

There is little published research on the overall history of combat stress. However, stressful events pre-date Christ, and it can be assumed that the same adverse psychological and emotional effects experienced today were also experienced then. It is only natural to assume that since the dawn of man, warriors have succumbed to fears. Even in the Stone Age it was human nature to have nightmares after a fearful day spent hunting vicious animals and dealing with other life-threatening situations.

"In 1000 BC, Hori, an Egyptian warrior, wrote about the feelings he experienced before going into battle, reflecting, 'You determine to go forward ... shuddering seizes you, the hair on your head stands on end, and your soul lies in your hand.'"[19]

Herodotus, the Greek historian, wrote about Leonidas, the Spartan commander and king of the Greek city of Sparta, who, at the battle of Thermopylae Pass in 480 BC, stopped his men from joining the combat because he recognized the troops were psychologically spent from previous battles. Leonidas wrote, "They had no heart for the fight and were unwilling to take their share of the danger."[20]

The idea of talk therapy attracted the attention of other Athenian intellectuals as well. The fifth century philosopher Gorgias recognized that although medicine cures diseases of the body, wisdom in the form of talking and teaching liberates the soul from sufferings.

Interestingly, "combat-related psychological and emotional stress existed more than 2000 years ago ... [yet] the idea that this suffering could be prevented by means of social conditioning

---

19   Ustinova, Yulia; Cardeña, Etzel , *Combat stress disorders and their treatment in ancient Greece. Psychological Trauma: Theory, Research, Practice, and Policy* Nov 1, 2014
20   Bentley, S. (2005, March 1). A Short History of PTSD: From Thermopylae to Hue Soldiers Have Always Had A Disturbing Reaction To War. Retrieved October 30, 2015, from http://www.vva.org/archive/TheVeteran/2005_03/feature_HistoryPTSD.htm

to war proved to be false."[21] No matter how much one trains for combat and is hardened in a military environment, he/she is still a human being and not a machine. When a comrade in arms is killed or injured, a warrior will experience strong feelings of loss that may lessen their combat effectiveness. This is why R&R is important: soldiers can spend time talking with each other and share personal concerns, letting one another know they have similar human emotional reactions to battle.

This early beginning of talk therapy described by Gorgias was the precursor to centuries of talk therapy, which is still effective today in helping troops and veterans with PTS. Even the ancient Greeks distinguished between medicine, which cured diseases, and talk therapy, which cured emotional effects of war. There are many examples in historical literature that describe the psychological difficulties that combat inflicts on war fighters. The classic novels *The Iliad* and *The Odyssey* are good examples of stories that discuss military battle and the adverse physical and psychological effects of combat stress in war.

To a certain degree, our present-day war fighters and their families are the same in many ways as past warriors.

While mythology reflects the horrors and psychological impact of war, it took many years for anyone to label this condition. In the 17th century, the term "nostalgia" was coined to describe the negative impact that occurs on soldiers who "enter military service and ... lose all hope of returning safely ... [which

---

21   Ustinova, Y., & Cardeña, E. (2014). Combat Stress Disorders and Their Treatment in Ancient Greece. Retrieved November 7, 2015, from http://www.researchgate.net/publication/269035855_Combat_Stress_Disorders_and_Their_Treatment_in_Ancient_Greece

eventually results in] indifference."[22] Then, during the Civil War, the name changed again when Dr. Jacob Mendez da Costa called soldiers' "increased arousal, irritability, and elevated heart rate … 'Soldier's Heart.'"[23]

An outstanding article, "Historical and Contemporary Perspectives of Combat Stress and the Army Combat Stress Control Team," written by CPT Bret Moore, Psy.D and CPT Greg Reger, PhD, discusses the fascinating history of combat stress. First, they cite 18th century author Leopold Auenbruger's description of combat stress: "When young men who are still growing are forced to enter military service and thus lose all hope of returning safe and returning to their beloved homeland, they become sad, taciturn, listless, solitary, musing, and full of sighs and moans. Finally, they cease to pay attention and become indifferent to everything, which the maintenance of life requires of them."[24] Fortunately, doctors looked to natural treatment, even as far back as the Civil War. For example, Dr. Costa found that "tonics," rest, and diet alleviated symptoms for many of the soldiers.

Auenbruger's accounts of what warfighters went through is consistent with what America's troops have experienced from the very beginning of our country's evolution. The diagnosis of "nostalgia" was given to Swiss soldiers in 1678 by Dr. Johannes

---

22 Moore, B., & Reger, G. (n.d.). Historical and Contemporary Perspectives of Combat Stress and the Army Combat Stress Control Team. Retrieved November 7, 2015, from http://stress.org/wp-content/uploads/2011/08/Historical-and-Contemporary-Perspectives-of-Combat-and-Operational-Stress.pdf

23 Phelps, A. (2015). PTSD in the Military. Retrieved November 7, 2015, from http://link.springer.com/referenceworkentry/10.1007/978-3-319-08613-2_80-1#page-1

24 Historical and Contemporary Perspectives of Combat Stress and the Army Combat Stress Control Team by CPT Bret A. Moore, Psy.D. & CPT Greg Reger, PhD

Hofer. During the Napoleonic wars, they prescribed cures for "nostalgia," such as exercise, listening to music, and general counseling; incidentally, this is consistent with what today is termed *integrative wellness*. From the Napoleonic wars up to the Civil War, most medical staff perceived combat stress reactions in a similar manner.

COMBAT STRESS IN THE CIVIL WAR AND BEYOND

Between the Civil War and WWI, the United States took part in several smaller military conflicts. These resulted in fewer casualties than the Civil War, yet the suffering, pain, and mental anguish were arguably the same. For example, the Western Indian Wars occurred shortly after the Civil War and were brutal in terms of the mayhem (i.e., torture, no-rules warfare, and guerilla fighting).

Conflict in the Philippines furthered the violence, along with the introduction of the devastating 1911 Colt semi-automatic pistol. Not only was this pistol used during the Spanish-American War—the war that made Teddy Roosevelt a hero—but it is still used today. However, no wars or conflicts came even close to exceeding the total overall deaths and destruction compared of "the war to end all wars" —World War I.

COMBAT STRESS IN WWI

America's involvement in World War I introduced a new name for combat stress—shell shock—which was one of the most accurate terms in that it reflected what was actually causing most of the combat stress trauma. World War I often included trench warfare, where thousands of miles of trenches were dug to hide and do battle. Soldiers were shoulder to shoulder in these trenches, and when they advanced to open ground, machine gun fire and a barrage of artillery shells would savagely cut them down. Artillery shells caused much more than 50 percent of all casualties in WWI. Hundreds of thousands of additional casualties were the result of poison gas, which was a first. With thousands of soldiers dying each day, it is estimated that about eight million soldiers from various countries died during this war.

When you consider the number of human beings from over forty countries who fought in WWI—approximately 60 million—and the incomprehensible number of deaths, one wonders how the world ever recovered mentally from the deadliest war in human history.

Fortunately for those troops, many countries created special programs for the citizens who fought in the war. In the United States, for instance, Congress' observations of the shockingly large numbers of the WWI veterans suffering from a variety of physical, emotional, and psychological ailments resulted in the enactment of the 1920 Vocational Rehabilitation Act, which led to the birth of the medical specialty of Physical Medicine and Rehabilitation (PM&R). Between the first and second world wars, PM&R came into its own. Veterans from WWI were helped in overcoming physical and mental problems with the goal of being returned to employment in their communities. In 1937, a new specialty was developed to further what already was being practiced, and the PM&R physician was now called a physiatrist (PM&R medical doctor.)

Another two decades would pass before the attack on Pearl Harbor, when the United States became involved in WWII. The name for the residual effects of combat stress changed again, this time from "combat neurosis" to "combat exhaustion" or "battle fatigue." During WWII, one out of four soldiers experienced some form of battle fatigue and, for a period of time, became ineffective and unable to fight. Overall, 25 percent of psychological casualties were caused by war trauma, and this rate was even higher—50 percent—for soldiers engaged in long, intense fighting, such as what was seen from D-Day in France through the end of the war in Germany.

So many soldiers were affected by battle stress that psychiatrists were confronted with the reality that psychological weakness had little to do with subsequent distress in combat.[25] The United States soon came to realize, due to the high number of battle fatigue casualties, that "every man and woman had a breaking point."[26]

25 Bentley, S. (2005). Short history of PTSD: From Thermopylae to Hue soldiers have always had a disturbing reaction to war. *Vietnam Veterans of America: The Veteran.* Retrieved from http://www.vva.org/archive/TheVeteran/2005_03/feature_HistoryPTSD.htm

26 Magee, D. (2006, May 15). PTSD: Only the name has changed. WCF Courier. Retrieved from http://wcfcourier.com/news/metro/ptsd-only-the-name-has-changed/article_394e-abda-6a67-5b42-ab5b-2643c4158f11.html

With this realization, more attention was paid to helping soldiers cope with trauma. Retired Colonel Frank Knudson revealed to me in an interview that that R&R, along with counseling with a Catholic Chaplin, worked for his crew when dealing with combat stress. More importantly, he and his crew received no meds during the R&R process.

During the Korean War, the approach to combat stress became even more focused. Due to the work and article by Albert Glass, MD, FAPA, titled *"Psychiatry in the U.S. Army: Lessons for Community Psychiatry,"* combat stress reactions were dealt with on an individual basis, which proved to be more successful in reducing the number of combat stress reactions.

Instead of using the ineffective prescreening processes from WWII, psychiatrists instead employed new procedures; they would rotate troops, and they would also evaluate patients "on a case-by-case basis"[27] With these new protocols, there were significantly less battle fatigue cases reported[28]—"during World War II, twenty-three percent of the evacuations were for psychiatric reasons; in Korea, psychiatric evacuations dropped to six percent."[29]

---

27   Kimball, B. (2008). Lesson 1: Introduction to Combat Stress. Retrieved October 31, 2015, from http://www.namb.net/WorkArea/linkit.aspx?LinkIdentifier=id&ItemID=8590121953&libID=8590121967

28   Kimball, B. (2008). Lesson 1: Introduction to Combat Stress. Retrieved October 31, 2015, from http://www.namb.net/WorkArea/linkit.aspx?LinkIdentifier=id&ItemID=8590121953&libID=8590121967

29   Bourne, P. (1970). Men, stress, and Vietnam. Boston: Little, Brown.

MOST CURRENT WARS USING THE TERM PTSD

A decade after Korea, the United States became embroiled in another conflict in Vietnam. The Department of Defense utilized similar mental health policies in Vietnam as in Korea, with soldiers generally deployed for one year before returning to United States. This rotation approach to avoid the aftermath of combat stress was not as effective in Vietnam as it had been in Korea due to the fact that soldiers in Vietnam were deployed as individuals rather than total units. The war took on significant political ramifications for the soldiers fighting in Southeast Asia and, making matters worse, the civilian population exhibited extraordinarily negative attitudes toward the returning soldiers.

In Dr. Brian M. Kimball's paper, "A 13-Week Bible Study," Kimball writes:

> Combat stress was a profound problem during the Vietnam War. Attempts were made to minimize the impact of battle fatigue, but these efforts actually made the problem worse. The rotation policy in the Korean War seemed to reduce battle fatigue casualties; so military planners believed that rotating soldiers individually would improve the morale of soldiers while maximizing the fighting ability of the unit. This plan seemed like a good idea, but actually made combat stress a greater problem because of the overwhelming absence of unit cohesion. This lack of cohesion created

a hostile environment, and the average soldier did not trust leadership.[30]

I personally experienced this same reaction of unit cohesion when I was the commanding officer of a general hospital unit section that was deployed during the first Persian Gulf War.

We had approximately 300 people in a U.S. Army Reserve hospital who had trained together for years—one weekend each month and two weeks a year. At times we were deployed for natural disasters such as earthquakes and hurricanes. When the unit was told they would deploy for a year, they were anxious but looked forward to serving together. When the final order arrived that they would be deployed individually, they were very unhappy and felt let down. Many soldiers stated that they trained together and knew each other, both in the military work environment and as an extended family—they even knew one another's spouses and children. Now they were being shipped out as individuals, not knowing whom they would be working with or where they would go. It was like starting from day one, establishing an involvement and trust with new colleagues. When they returned after one year, there were all kinds of family, employment, and military problems.

If they had been deployed as a group, these problems most likely would not have occurred to the extent they did; there would have been a camaraderie, both among deployed soldiers in their assigned military duties and their families back home.

30   Kimball, B. (2008). Lesson 1: Introduction to Combat Stress. Retrieved October 31, 2015, from http://www.namb.net/WorkArea/linkit.aspx?LinkIdentifier=id&ItemID=8590121953&libID=8590121967

Many hospital staff, returning from deployment, stated they felt the Army had no heart in the way they deployed members of our general hospital.

In Vietnam, not only were soldiers not deployed together, but total units were not rotated out of battle together but rather as individuals. Within a day or two of leaving battle, soldiers were back home in the company of people who had not fought with them and did not share their experiences. That is why today there are still veteran support groups made up of Vietnam vets that shared the same or similar deployment. They share with each other now what they didn't have an opportunity to discuss when they were initially discharged. Whether this retelling of past stories is now constructive or not is a question only the vet can answer.

Another stressor Vietnam vets experienced was the mood of the country when returning from combat. There were demonstrations against the Vietnam War and some of the citizenry was not hospitable to vets whom they encountered. I personally recall when I was in uniform at the end of the Vietnam War in San Francisco, being treated very poorly by many civilians in the city. This was a war that many people felt we lost, even though I know of no major battle we did not win there. The general media and politicians created an environment that had never existed after past wars. The combination of the above factors has resulted in Vietnam vets still being treated for PTSD forty years after the war ended.

When I was working with Vietnam vets at Tripler Army Medical Center they were being labeled as having "Vietnam Post-traumatic stress disorder." There were other terms used, but by 1980 the American Psychiatric Association officially recognized the sole term PTSD as a mental health disorder in the Diagnostic and Statistical Manual-III-Revised (DSM III R – now DSM V). This directly stated that post-traumatic stress (PTS) was no longer seen as a normal reaction to being in an abnormal environment, as it had been in preceding decades, but rather as a disorder and chemical imbalance of the brain. (The DSM is psychiatry's diagnostic manual, which labels people as being mentally ill).

Although generally accepted in the medical field and by the general public as a scientifically derived diagnostic tool, there actually is no real hard science associated with any mental disorder in the DSM. That is to say that there is no medical test— including X-rays, MRIs, CAT scans, or urine or blood tests—that can reveal an objective, confirmable abnormality of the brain. Psychiatric diagnosing is completely based on the subjective opinions of mental health professionals (primarily psychiatrists) who meet every so many years and decide how to label people. Then the pharmaceutical companies rush to develop a drug for each new label.

As a result of having a psychiatric label, many veterans believed that their reactions to combat were abnormal and therefore entitled them to receive military disability benefits despite having no medical data to support an actual brain abnormality. They also began to be treated with dangerous brain-altering psychiatric medications that made it very difficult for them to return to normal functioning.

Since the Persian Gulf wars, combatants have extensively been treated both at home and on the battlefield with never before seen levels of psychiatric medications. It all started with the labeling in the APA's DSM.

SO WHAT IS THE DIFFERENCE BETWEEN COMBAT STRESS AND PTSD?

The residual effects of combat stress can include a range of behaviors that result from the extreme stress of battle. Some common symptoms are depression, fatigue, inability to focus, slower reaction times, indecision, disconnection from one's family and general every day surroundings, and inability to use good judgment. These individual or combined combat stress reactions most likely can be short-term and should not be labeled as a disorder. This is PTS, a normal reaction to an abnormal situation (even in the civilian community, the results of an unusual life-threatening experience can produce similar symptoms temporarily).

PTS accompanied by the "disorder," on the other hand, is experienced over a longer period of time than combat stress or PTS. PTSD occurs when an individual is unable to adjust to civilian life and return to normal; it often occurs when a soldier does not have adequate time to recover before returning to his/her community and family. Even with adequate time (during WWII it could have been months before returning to the civilian community), the individual may need professional help to figure out how to normalize himself or herself. It is not unusual that long-term disorders, attributable to combat stress, may commence as combat stress' residual effects. It seems fair to say that based on the history of combat, available data, and years of experience, it is likely that 99% of troops, having seen combat, will experience, to varying degrees, some form of PTS. There also are cases (perhaps one percent) of troops who may not experience any form of PTS whatsoever, be in denial about the experience, or have had severe mental issues prior to being deployed.

THE UTILIZATION OF BRAIN-ALTERING MEDICATIONS AND CONTRASTING INTEGRATIVE TREATMENT

When returning either home or back to duty, troops need to understand that any type of brain-altering drug, either legal or illegal, significantly interferes with getting back to normal. In order to make the transition back to normal living and interpersonal relations, the mind must be clear and devoid of any type of brain-altering medication or substance. Too often soldiers will self-medicate, believing these legal and illegal substances will relieve the normal reaction to combat stress.

A friend, retired USMC Brigadier General, David Brahms, Esq., is an attorney who represents an increasing number of Marines from the Marine Corps Base Camp Pendleton for a variety of reasons, ranging from being inappropriately discharged from the military to criminal offenses while on active duty. Gen. Brahms is the prototypical Marine general, tall and trim with a booming voice. He believed a young Marine was being unjustly discharged and, in his distinct New England accent, requested my immediate assistance at his office to conduct a psychological evaluation. Based on the general's experience with returning troops suffering from combat stress, he believed the Marine had never been evaluated for PTS. Upon meeting the Marine, a psychological evaluation was conducted and a considerable amount of time was spent talking with the Marine's wife.

The Marine had returned several months earlier from a combat tour in Iraq and had been fulfilling his stateside military duty. During this time he began experiencing hypervigilance, nightmares, delusional thinking, and depression, resulting in his inability to return to the "normal" he had known prior to his deployment. The Marine explained that he was having nightmares, which, at times, resulted in his jumping out of bed and seeking shelter. Upon further explanation, he said the nearby amusement park had a regularly scheduled fireworks display and it was at this time that he felt the need to seek shelter.

The Marine further explained that when entering a restaurant, or any public facility, he sought out a seating area where he was able to sit with his back next to a wall and explained that the sight of a Catholic or Protestant church would automatically appear as a mosque. Although he was able to return to duty, when returning from the base to his home each day, he became very solemn and inactive. This is a very different picture than what his life was like prior to his combat duty. Throughout high school he had been a star athlete, and he came from a good, stable, family. Now he was gaining weight, had become extremely lethargic, and was more or less in a daily funk. There was no history of any illegal drug use and he had never been diagnosed with any type of mental illness.

In an effort to return to his normal routine, the Marine, based on what he heard about athletes using steroids, had decided to take a steroid; he'd hoped it would jumpstart his life and get him back to being the athlete and, more importantly, the husband he had been before deployment. Although his wife was a well-educated professional, he convinced her to go along with this plan. She was hopeful that the steroids would return her husband to the normal he, and she, had known before deployment. The Marine made the mistake of using an illegal steroid, injecting it into his leg. Within twenty-four hours he sought medical assistance on base, complaining of a severe cold.

While the physician was examining him for potential respiratory problems, the Marine explained that he was experiencing a problem with his leg, admitting to the physician that he had injected a steroid the day before. Rather than refer him for mental health services, the physician called his commanding officer, recommending a discharge from the corps. This was a gung-ho Marine whose life revolved around the corps with the hope and belief he would eventually retire after twenty years of service. The Marine was further devastated by the thought of being dishonorably discharged from a vocation that meant so much to him. He became more depressed and potentially suicidal, believing life, as he knew it, was over. He seemed completely unaware of the reasons behind his abnormal behavior—unaware that the behaviors he described, such as hypervigilance, nightmares, and depression, were normal reactions to abnormal experiences of the combat environment. With each symptom he described, it became clear that these were classic signs of PTS, and it was explained to him that what he was experiencing was normal. The Marine was unaware of any similar emotional or behavioral problems among his peers, and he believed they were unaware of the problems he was experiencing and even believed that he was doing "great." This is a classic case of post-traumatic stress that turned into a disorder. The Marine was experiencing continual stress and trauma from his combat experience and, unknowingly, allowed it to change his life for the worse.

In an effort to help him move back into his normal routine, detailed information was provided to him about the various techniques necessary for dealing with his debilitating symptoms. A detailed evaluation was provided to General Brahms, who forwarded the diagnosis of PTSD, along with the recommended treatment, to the Marine's commanding officer. The charges were dropped and the Marine was allowed to remain in the service, pursuing the recommended treatment described in my report.

This is not a unique case by any means, which was illustrated during a radio show on the topic covered by Daniel Zwerdling and Michael De Yolanna on Colorado Public radio. In their broadcast, they stated: "The U.S. Army has kicked out more than 22,000 soldiers since 2009 for 'misconduct,' after they returned from Iraq and Afghanistan and were diagnosed with mental health disorders and traumatic brain injuries. That means many of those soldiers are not receiving the crucial treatment or retirement and health care benefits they would have received with an honorable discharge."[31]

The overall reason for many of the discharges was "misconduct," which can include everything from excessive drinking to anger/hostility or irresponsible behavior. Just about all the behaviors identified as misconduct are consistent with the adverse effects of brain-altering psychiatric medications.

The above discussion never states that psychiatric brain-altering medications indicate potential suicide ideation, poor judgment/reasoning, anger, hostility, and depression as possible side effects. However, many of these behaviors are consistent with Zwerdling and Yolanna's descriptions of the vets they interviewed when doing their research.

There is some evidence from the discussion that may indicate that these troops were on psych meds, as patients made comments such as: "I can't do it, Sir, I'm … losing my mind, like last night I just wanted to … take all my pills … This is killing me, physically and mentally," and "I had one doctor saying, 'Oh, you just got some anxiety; here's some sleeping medication and antidepressants. You'll be fine.'"[32]

---

31   Thousands Of Soldiers With Mental Health Disorders Kicked Out For 'Misconduct' (n.d.). Retrieved November 21, 2015, from http://www.npr.org/sections/thetwo-way/2015/10/28/452652731/thousands-of-soldiers-with-mental-health-disorders-kicked-out-for-misconduct
32   Thousands Of Soldiers With Mental Health Disorders Kicked Out For 'Misconduct' (n.d.). Retrieved November 21, 2015, from http://www.npr.org/sections/thetwo-way/2015/10/28/452652731/thousands-of-soldiers-with-mental-health-disorders-kicked-out-for-misconduct

I have evaluated many Marines who were going to be kicked out of the military for similar reasons and, with the assistance of a lawyer, succeeded in keeping their post, as well as getting appropriate integrative treatment.

This is a huge problem that is not being handled correctly and won't until formal, military-wide, standardized integrative treatment programs are developed without brain-altering medications. I know one of the psychiatrists cited in the previous story, and she stated that these vets needed to be kept in the military and not discharged; unfortunately, she was also one of the primary psychiatrists who implemented the plan of psych meds at home as well as on the battlefield.

We need to recognize the value of physiatrists dealing with this problem rather than psychiatrists, whose primary treatment modality is brain-altering psychiatric medication, which makes the problem worse—especially for soldiers with TBIs.

Treatment without medication is consistent with what happened to so many veterans returning from World War II, Korea, and Vietnam. World War II bomber pilot Colonel Frank Knudsen is a good example of healing from the trauma of war without the use of psychiatric drugs.

In 2014, I interviewed Knudsen, who represents a successful transition from combat to a normal, productive civilian life. Knudsen, 94 years old at the time of the interview, piloted B-25s and B-17s during World War II, followed that up as an A-26 pilot during the Korean conflict and, amazingly, even flew transport planes in Vietnam and flew B-52's with the U.S. Strategic Command afterward.

Knudsen had been with the 22nd Bomber Group during WWII, initially flying out of North Africa and Italy. Later, he flew missions out of Great Britain and throughout Europe, including Germany, logging a total of forty-four missions by the end of the war.

Knudsen arrived in North Africa with his bomber crew on D-Day and, despite initially being scheduled to land that day in Italy, the flight was detoured to North Africa because of the eruption of Mount Vesuvius, which had literally covered the runway with three feet of ash. As a result of the initial diversion, Knudsen and his crew flew many of the early bombing missions out of North Africa, with his most memorable being the targeting of the Nazi oil refinery fields in Ploesti, Romania.

The missions over Romania were extremely dangerous, not only because Knudsen was forced to fly through the Alps, rather than over them, due to the 1800-feet altitude limitation of his B-25, but also because these were the missions where his only flight plan consisted of a single sheet of paper with crude drawings to assist him in navigating the treacherous turns within the mountains.

Getting to the target was the easy part. Once in Romania, Nazi Luftwaffe fighters and anti-aircraft guns had to be avoided long enough to accurately drop the bomb load before immediately turning around and beginning, again, the nail-biting navigation through the Alps toward home base.

Knudsen reminisced about the devastatingly large number of casualties on these missions. During World War II, more airmen were killed than Marines or sailors; the following data may explain why it was such an achievement for Knudsen to survive forty-four remarkable bombing missions.

Due to what Frank Knudsen told me about his experiences, I researched this further; in the World Heritage Encyclopedia, I discovered that:

"The United States Army Air Forces incurred 12% of the Army's 936,000 battle casualties in World War II. 88,119 airmen died in service. 52,173 were battle casualty deaths: 45,520 killed in action, 1,140 died of wounds, 3,603 were missing in action and declared dead, and 1,910 were non-hostile battle deaths. Of the United States military and naval services, only the Army Ground Forces suffered more battle deaths. 35,946 non-battle deaths included 25,844 in aircraft accidents, more than half of which occurred within the Continental United States."[33]

Knudsen watched many of his buddies, flying in formation, get hit with shrapnel and explode. A memory, even today, that is difficult for Knudsen to recall.

There is little doubt that the airmen filling the skies over Europe and the Pacific witnessed combat situations that would emotionally and psychologically challenge anyone in similar circumstances. How did those who survived handle the trauma of the war?

---

33 World Heritage Encyclopedia. (2014). Retrieved October 31, 2015, from http://www.worldheritage.org/articles/U.S.AAF

Knudsen's immediate sarcastic response was that on the first mission his crews "were all atheists." After returning from subsequent missions, each and every member of the crew became true believers in God. Upon return to "terra firma," they kissed the ground and together said Hail Marys. The statement, "There are no atheists in foxholes" was never truer than it was for Knudsen and his crews.

Having survived thirty-three missions, Knudsen and his crew returned to the United States for reassignment or discharge, spending three months in North Carolina preparing to make the transition to either civilian life or reassignment. Knudsen recalls that neither he nor his crew were ever given psychiatric medication but did, in fact, spend a good deal of time with a Catholic priest, praying and talking. There was much discussion of what was experienced during combat and also an equal amount of discussion about hopes and dreams once the war ended.

According to Knudsen, after the three months all of the members of his crew either returned home or on to future deployment. Each dealt with their stress during the three months of R&R in North Carolina and moved on with their life.

To confirm Knudsen and his crew experienced PTS, one only need review the casualty numbers above. The successful treatment approach to deal with combat stress was interpersonal counseling with someone Knudsen, and his crew, trusted, as well as peer support.

Thankfully for Knudsen and many others, during and after WWII, they weren't labeled as mentally ill and subjected to dangerous mind-altering drugs. They simply were recognized as having a normal reaction to the abnormal circumstances of combat.

The following are criteria listed in the current DSM for diagnosing PTSD:

> Exposure to actual or threatened death, serious injury, or sexual violence in one (or more) of the following ways: (1) Directly experiencing the traumatic event … (2) Witnessing the event … (3) Learning that the traumatic event(s) occurred to a close family member or close friend … [or] (4)Experiencing repeated or extreme exposure to aversive details of the traumatic event.[34]

Knudsen and his crew experienced many of the symptoms described above in the DSM but were never diagnosed as having a disorder; they were simply given three months of rest and relaxation, as well as effective talk therapy with not only a priest, but also time among themselves to openly talk about their experiences. Unlike Knudsen and his crew, combat veterans today are not provided appropriate time, or treatment, to readjust, making the smooth transition back into the neighborhood a near-impossibility. Knudsen and his crew were no different than all the warriors who went before them, experiencing fear, trauma, and stress from combat situations. The difference is, however, the manner in which they were healed.

---

34   The DSM 5's New PTSD Diagnostic Criteria. (n.d.). Retrieved November 19, 2015, from http://navwaters.com/2013/06/14/the-dsm-5s-new-ptsd-diagnostic-criteria/.

Finally, I have a close friend who was a POW in Vietnam for 7 1/2 years. He echoed to me his experience with the 3 Rs when he returned to the United States at the end of the Vietnam War. He stated that he was given three months by the military to rest and relax before being reassigned to duty. Over these three months he did not take any type of psychiatric medication but basically visited with family and friends and enjoyed his three-month vacation. These three months represent the third "R," recovery time.

The biggest issue with today's soldier is not their inability to function on the battlefield, but their difficulty returning to the civilian community. The United States has the best trained and supplied military in the world due to extensive training to prepare soldiers for combat. As I can attest with my own personal training to become a combat engineer, I was well trained and hardened to do my job and survive on the battlefield. But as good as the preparation for combat was, the preparation for a return to civilian life was very much lacking.

For years I have recommended to state and federal lawmakers and military officials to institute a comprehensive transitional program. As history shows, the warriors of today share the detrimental effects of battle with those who went before them. As history further reveals, there are successful, more compassionate methods of treatment that don't involve dangerous brain-altering drugs.

Therefore, the current focus of research should not be on physically altering what is a normal reaction to stress in combat, but to examine a person's total readiness for deployment, i.e., leaving their family, job, friends, and relatives. Also, the military should develop meaningful, extended re-integrative programs for when a soldier returns from their deployment. No soldier should ever be discharged from the military with the label of a disorder, no matter how long it takes him or her to recover and return to normal functioning.

From my basic anatomy and physiology college courses I have learned that the autonomic nervous system (ANS) is an unconsciously acting control that regulates specific bodily functions such as the heart rate, digestion, respiratory rate, pupillary response, urination, and sexual arousal. This ANS is the primary mechanism in control of the fight-or-flight response that has, since the beginning of time, kept the human species from becoming extinct. It is a division of the peripheral nervous system that influences the function of internal organs.

The autonomic nervous system has two distinct branches: the sympathetic nervous system (SNS) and the parasympathetic nervous system (PSNS). The sympathetic nervous system triggers the fight-or-flight response, while the parasympathetic nervous system is responsible for reinstating normal functioning. Each system balances the other, with the SNS activating a physiological response and the PSNS inhibiting a response.

With the above in mind, one may have a better understanding of a person who experiences chronic stress, as seen in combat deployments. The activation of the SNS results in the release of hormones, i.e. cortisol, endorphins, and adrenaline, which serves to enable a person to survive in a fight-or-flight environment.

Continuous stress causes long-term effects on the brain and body that can continue to impact a soldier long after they return from combat. For example, stress raises the level of cortisol, a hormone that improves concentration briefly during acute stressful situations (hypervigilance). However, cortisol damages the hippocampus when brain levels remain high for an extended period of time. Since the hippocampus is the part of the brain where information is stored and retrieved, damage to this area of the brain can result in memory problems.

There are many other residual effects of constant stress that affects a person's physical and mental well-being if constructive steps are not taken to help the soldier return to a more normal status by balancing the SNS and the PSNS.

CHAPTER 3

SUICIDES AND HOMICIDES WITHIN THE ARMED FORCES AND CIVILIAN COMMUNITY: A DIRECT LINK TO PSYCHIATRIC MEDICATIONS

The 2010 report of the Army Suicide Prevention Task Force found: "Suicide rates in the military were traditionally lower than among civilians in the same age range, but in 2004 the suicide rate in the U.S. Army began to climb, surpassing the civilian rate in 2008. Substance use is involved in many of these suicides."

They also found that:

29 percent of active duty Army suicides from FY 2005 to FY 2009 involved alcohol or drug use; and in 2009, prescription drugs were involved in almost one third of the suicides. However, in spite of the low level of illicit drug use in the military, abuse of prescription drugs is higher among service members than among civilians and is on the increase. In 2008, 11 percent of service members reported misusing prescription drugs, up from 2 percent in 2002 and 4 percent in 2005.[35]

I observe that misuse is not the only problem; many service members are given multiple psychiatric medications by their psychiatrist that, in combination, have disastrous side effects (i.e. suicide, sudden death, and homicide). The biggest problem is that veterans are accustomed to following orders and doing whatever their doctor instructs. Although one can read the significant *black box warnings* on the side effects of a single psychiatric medication, no one knows the side effects of multiple psychiatric medications. It's like playing Russian roulette, except the gun is always pointed at the veteran's head.

The fact that prescription drugs were involved in one third of the military suicides is no coincidence; "Use of psychiatric medications in the military increased almost 700% from 2005 through 2011."[36] The first black box warning on these psychiatric medications is suicidality.

---

35 Executive Summary. (n.d.). Retrieved October 31, 2015, from http://www.stripes.com/pol-opoly_fs/1.115776.1282666756!/menu/standard/file/Suicide Prevention Task Force_EXEC SUM_08-20-10 v6.pdf
36 Friedman, R. (2013, April 6). Wars on Drugs. Retrieved October 31, 2015, from http://www.nytimes.com/2013/04/07/opinion/sunday/wars-on-drugs.html

Over the past decade, there has been an epidemic of suicides among active duty personnel and veterans. Despite overwhelming data supporting a link between the increased use of psychiatric medications and suicide, little to no action by lawmakers and/or the military has been taken to reduce the number of psychiatric medications being prescribed as treatment.

An organization that works for Mental Health Human Rights (Citizens Commission on Human Rights International (CCHR)), has done extensive research on suicides in the military and made a documentary called "Hidden Enemy: Inside Psychiatry's Covert Agenda." In this documentary they provided factual information that cannot be ignored. In early 2013, according to the United States Department of Defense and U.S. Department of Veterans' Affairs, "the number of military suicides in 2012 had far exceeded the total of those killed in battle—an average of nearly one a day ... [and] veteran suicide was running at 22 a day—about 8000 a year."[37]

Though some people believe "self-harm ... [results from wartime stress] the facts reveal that 85% of military suicides have not seen combat—and 52% never even deployed."[38] The claim that self-harm is due to stress of war is inconsistent with the above information; it is also inconsistent with what I have discovered regarding prisoners of war (POWs) in Vietnam.

---

37   The Hidden Enemy Documentary Exposes the Covert Operation Behind Military Suicides. (n.d.). Retrieved October 31, 2015, from http://www.cchr.org/documentaries/the-hidden-enemy.html
38   The Hidden Enemy Documentary Exposes the Covert Operation Behind Military Suicides. (n.d.). Retrieved October 31, 2015, from http://www.cchr.org/documentaries/the-hidden-enemy.html

Arthur "Neil" Black was a POW for seven and a half years in the Vietnam War, where he was held at the Hanoi Hilton. I have known Neil for over forty years and asked him how many of his fellow POWs committed suicide while in captivity. One would expect that the life-and-death stresses they experienced would result in a number of individuals breaking down and committing suicide. Similar stresses were portrayed in the 2014 theatrical release *Unbroken*, which depicted the brutality experienced by Lewis "Louie" Zamperini at the hands of a Japanese officer called "Bird" who repeatedly abused Louie in an attempt to break his spirit.

Neil explained to me that their Vietnam captors were every bit as brutal as Bird. When I asked Neil to provide me with suicide statistics for Vietnam POWs, he went to the POW Association Historian and provided me with the following: Of all the 800 POWs (662 of U.S. military got out alive and 138 civilians/ foreign nationals got out alive). Another 72, listed, died in captivity ... none due to suicide.[39]

One immediately asks themselves, how can this be true? My answer to this question is that none of the POWs in Vietnam were on any type of brain-altering psychiatric medications. They possessed normal brains that were instrumental in their survival, even in light of the constant daily threat of being tortured and executed. Their normal brain allowed them to develop all sorts of communication techniques with each other and a closeness that will be unparalleled for the remainder of their life.

---

39   Defense POW/MIA Accounting Agency. (n.d.). Retrieved November 19, 2015, from
      http://www.dpaa.mil/Home.aspx

In Chapter 9, I will discuss in detail the strong psychological need that human beings possess for love and belonging. This need was met to its maximum by these prisoners of war when they were dependent on each other for support and survival. Again, communication and a strong sense of involvement carried the day and resulted in not one POW committing suicide while in captivity.

Taking the above example of Vietnam POWs surviving with no suicides, one wonders why both military and civilian psychiatrists are widening the definitions of what it means to be "mentally ill" in their Diagnostic And Statistic Manual (DSM), especially when it comes to post-traumatic stress disorder (PTSD) in soldiers and in veterans. In psychiatry, diagnoses of psychological disorders such as PTSD, personality disorder, and social anxiety disorder are almost inevitably followed by the prescription of at least one psychiatric drug. The example above illustrates quite clearly that close interpersonal involvement with a caring person, without brain altering drugs, is an effective way to avoid suicide.

It appears that people are beginning to recognize the importance of funding mental health agencies and organizations. "The U.S. Pentagon now spends $2 billion a year on mental health. The Veterans Administration's mental health budget has skyrocketed from less than $3 billion in 2007 to nearly $7 billion in 2014."[40]

---

40   The Hidden Enemy Documentary Exposes the Covert Operation Behind Military Suicides. (n.d.). Retrieved October 31, 2015, from http://www.cchr.org/documentaries/the-hidden-enemy.html

THE MILITARY CAN BE AN IDEAL FAMILY FOR SUICIDE PREVENTION

Suicides in the military have always been a major concern. The Department of Defense has issued orders to reduce the number of suicides in the military. Actually, there have been military commanding officers that issue orders for zero tolerance of suicides. On the surface, these orders seem to be unachievable, but based on the nature of our military's organizational charts, zero-tolerance would appear to be a realistic goal. The main problem that exists today in the military, and government in general, is that suicides in the military are compared with suicides in the general population. There have been times over the past twenty years that the general population exceeded suicides in the military and other times when military suicides not only exceeded suicides in the general population but has exceeded deaths in combat. My view is that the number of suicides in our military should be extremely low due to the way our military is structured. In the example below, you'll see how the military has the potential to operate like a family and how this structure can prevent suicides as long as each member of the "family" is held accountable for the consequences of their actions.

In the basic military organization, we have the smallest group of people (approx. 10 - 12) being in a squad. Each squad has a squad leader. Each squad is part of a platoon, where you generally have 4 Squads. Each platoon (approximately 4) is part of a company and each company (approx. 4), is part of a battalion. For the sake of this example, military members will be abbreviated as follows:

Squad members (SM)
Squad leader (SL)
First sergeant (Top)
Platoon leader (PL)
Company commander (CC)
Battalion commander (BC)

Ideal family structure:

This family consists of a mother, father, grandmother, and grandfather, along with several children in the family all working in the same family business. The mother, father, and several children live in the same house or neighborhood with the grandmother and grandfather living nearby. The family knows each member intimately; they know when other members are happy and when they're sad. The oldest brother (SL) oversees all his brothers and sisters (SM) chores. He is always aware of their feelings toward their jobs, as well as how they function in the family. The oldest brother and his mother (Top) are constantly aware of each of the children's health, both physical and mental, as well as their overall view of the world. The father (PL) is in charge of the household, and is intimately aware of his own children's thoughts and feelings, and all of the other employees (other SM) in his company, who are related family members such as cousins, and nephews.

The grandmother (CC) and grandfather (BC) constantly monitor and talk with the mother and father and, although they do not live in the same house, they visit often since they live nearby. When the mother and father have a problem with the children, they turn to the grandparents for support.

If even one child in the family has a problem, the whole family, including all the brothers, sisters, mother, father, grandmother, and grandfather, knows about it and is there to provide immediate help and direction. Every member of the family is supportive and marshals all their resources to help the one person who is experiencing difficulty. If, for example, child Jimmy is having a physical health or mental health issue, they immediately ensure that he is seen by the correct doctor, who just so happens to be one of the uncles in the family, where all uncles are doctors.

Let's say Jimmy lost a friend to a tragic car accident. Jimmy played baseball with this close friend and is depressed by the loss. When he sees his uncle doctor, the uncle only spends ten minutes with Jimmy and gives him psychiatric medication to help with the depression. When Jimmy wants to talk about the loss, his psychiatrist uncle states he does not have time to talk since he needs to see three or four more patients. Jimmy goes home and tells the family about this uncle's treatment. They notice when Jimmy takes these pills, he starts to complain about feeling like a zombie. The family also notices unusual behavior not consistent with Jimmy. The family calls another uncle, who is a psychologist, and when Jimmy sees him, his second uncle explains that feeling down after losing a friend who was killed is a normal reaction and that with time and the support of his family, he will feel better. The uncle takes away his psychiatric medication and tells him to move on with his life and schedules a second appointment to continue the talk therapy. The first uncle doctor was immediately disowned from the family for not caring and helping a fellow family member. The family held him accountable when he failed them.

In a sense, this is how the military should be set up. Each member of the squad is aware of all other members in the squad. The squad leader is not only aware of each member's status, but also responsible to ensure that all issues are resolved. The first sergeant meets with all the squad leaders to offer any assistance and training needed for the well-being of the total platoon. The platoon leader not only meets with the squad leaders but also the first sergeant.

The overall responsibility and training for the well-being of the platoon is in the hands of the platoon leader, who goes to the company commander for any assistance needed. If the company commander cannot come up with a solution for a problem, he goes to the battalion commander for the necessary assistance. The military organization's job is to keep one another alive and ensure that physical and mental health needs are being met. The problem now in the military is that the doctors who are not resolving the problems of the large numbers of suicides in the military are not being disowned.

With this close-knit military family there should be an awareness of every member in the organization by each other and especially by the senior person in charge; this could head off any thoughts or actual acts of suicide by making sure military personal receive the correct referral for help. If the appropriate help is not provided, then people up the chain of command should take corrective action. Just as they would in battle, the military has the structure to be a real-life family, but military leadership is not living up to its responsibilities to eliminate suicides,

An example of what I have been stating for years on the above subject can be seen in a seminar I gave for faculty and students, including veterans, on April 13, 2012 at a community college in San Marcos, California. The lecture identified how we can reduce the number of suicides by developing more integrative wellness programs for our vets and families. This talk is a good overview regarding my impressions on PTSD, TBI, and related suicides and homicides. I was asked to give this seminar because the faculty was apprehensive about how to treat veterans, and students in general, whom they suspect may have mental health issues. Due to the large number of veterans committing suicide, the faculty was very concerned about how to deal with potential problems. It was especially important to give faculty and staff insights as to what to look for and how to avoid and best deal with potential problems.

Shortly after the seminar, an article appeared in the New York Times (June 9, 2012). The title of the article was "Suicides Outpacing War Deaths for Troops" by Timothy Williams.[41] Williams' states:

---

41   Williams, T. (2012, June 8). Suicides Outpacing War Deaths for Troops. Retrieved October
31, 2015, from http://www.nytimes.com/2012/06/09/us/suicides-eclipse-war-deaths-for-us-troops.html

INVISIBLE SCARS

[The] suicide rate among the United States active duty military personnel has spiked in 2012, eclipsing the number of troops dying in battle, and is on pace to set a record annual high since the start of the wars in Iraq and Afghanistan. Although the United States military has withdrawn from Iraq and stepped up efforts to provide mental health, drug, and alcohol, as well as financial counseling services, suicides have increased. In June 2012, the military stated that there had been 154 suicides among active-duty troops, a rate of nearly one each day so far this year. The Associated Press first reported the figures in June 2012. That number represents an 18 percent increase over the 130 active-duty military suicides for the same period in 2011. There were 123 suicides from January to early June in 2010, and 133 during that period in 2009, the Pentagon said. By contrast, there were 124 American military fatalities in Afghanistan as of June 1, 2012, according to the Pentagon.

Suicide rates of military personnel and combat veterans have risen sharply since 2005, as the wars in Iraq and Afghanistan intensified. What Timothy Williams didn't report on was that between 2005 and 2011, a DoD report stated that DoD increased their purchase of psychiatric medications by almost 700%.[42]

In 2012, Paul Rieckhoff, the executive director of Iraq and Afghanistan Veterans of America, called suicides among active-

---

42   4 Richard A. Friedman, "War on Drugs," The New York Times, 6 Apr 2013; http://www.nytimes.com/2013/04/07/opinion/sunday/wars-ondrugs.html?ref=opinion&_r=0&g-wh=7E028A441FC225E6745B9904CFDA2A92&gwt=pay

duty military personnel "the tip of the iceberg." He cited a survey the group conducted that year among its 160,000 members that found that "37 percent knew someone who had committed suicide."[43]

As of January 18, 2015, the DoD's annual report showed "mixed outcomes for 2013. They stated a decline in active duty suicides (259) but an increase in Reserve and National Guard forces (220)."[44]

Although the DoD gave common characteristics among 2013 suicides, there was no mention regarding how many of these veterans were taking psychiatric medications. They listed several commonalities among these men and women, including "vets younger than 30, failed relationships, legal problems, and medical issues as common characteristics of veterans experiencing suicidal thoughts."[45]

In 2012, the DoD held a conference regarding suicides in the military, and psychiatric medications again were never considered to be the culprit.

In 2015, the U.S. Congress passed the "Clay Hunt Suicide Prevention for American Veterans Act." If one reads the actual act, they will see that it plans to "begin a student loan repay-

---

43   Williams, T. (2012, June 8). Suicides Outpacing War Deaths for Troops. Retrieved October 31, 2015, from http://www.nytimes.com/2012/06/09/us/suicides-eclipse-war-deaths-for-us-troops.html

44   Kovach, G. (2015, January 16). Love, war lead to military suicides. Retrieved October 31, 2015, from http://www.sandiegouniontribune.com/news/2015/jan/16/military-suicide-report-2013/

45   Kovach, G. (2015, January 16). Love, war lead to military suicides. Retrieved October 31, 2015, from http://www.sandiegouniontribune.com/news/2015/jan/16/military-suicide-report-2013/

ment pilot program that is aimed to attract, conscript, and retain psychiatrists."[46] While the intention of the act is good, the implementation is misguided. We should not be hiring more psychiatrists; psychiatrists are responsible for the over-prescription of dangerous drugs.

In 2012, the Associated Press reported the following:

> 154 suicides among active duty personnel as of June 3, 2012, nearly one a day for the year and 24 more than occurred between Jan. 1 to June 3, 2011. According to AP and service figures, the Marine Corps and Army have seen a slight uptick, with the Marine Corps having 18, the Army, 80. The Air Force has seen a sharp increase, up 32 from 23 at the same time last year. The Navy has seen a slight dip after experiencing a rising trend in the past few years ... [and] data from 2010 indicate it [suicide] is now the 10th leading cause of death of Americans, up from the 11th leading cause ... [while] in 2010 and 2011, suicide supplanted automobile and motorcycle accidents as the second leading cause of death for active duty personnel.[47]

One should know that brain-altering psychiatric drug therapy stands as one of the most significant perils to health, resulting in very serious adverse reactions in many people.

---

46   Horn, M. (2015, February 3). Senate passes, and Obama will sign, anti-suicide bill to aid vets. Retrieved October 31, 2015, from http://www.mcclatchydc.com/news/politics-government/congress/article24779593.html
47   Kime, P. (2012, June 15). DoD conference to address military suicides. Retrieved November 1, 2015, from http://archive.militarytimes.com/article/20120615/NEWS/206150310/

Not only should we be cautious about psychiatric medication, but it's also important to be aware that adverse drug reactions (ADR) from prescription drugs of all varieties is the fourth leading cause of death in the U.S. In any given month, 48 percent of U.S. consumers ingested a prescription drug, and 11% ingested five or more prescription drugs. Americans suffer from an estimated 45-50 million adverse effects from prescription drugs, of which 2.5 million to 4 million are serious, disabling, or fatal.[48]

DANGEROUS SIDE EFFECTS

Dr. Moira Dolan, a physician with the Medical Accountability Network, has this to say about antidepressants such as Prozac: "There are numerous examples of people who have gone on a shooting rampage and killed their classmates, their co-workers, members of their family and often took their own lives. It was shortly discovered that they were taking an antidepressant. The appearance is that the person was mentally ill and went on a rage but when these cases have actually been looked at closer, what we find is that the person did not have any violent tendencies and in most cases was not even suicidal before they started treatment with their antidepressant medication."[49]

She goes on to explain that these drug's labels have warnings that alert the user to the potential effect of "akathisia," meaning that

---

48   Preventable Adverse Drug Reactions: A Focus on Drug Interactions. (2014, June 18). Retrieved November 1, 2015, from http://www.fda.gov/Drugs/DevelopmentApprovalProcess/DevelopmentResources/DrugInteractionsLabeling/ucm110632.htm
49   The connection between violence, suicide, homicide, and antidepressants. (n.d.). Retrieved November 7, 2015, from http://www.encognitive.com/node/886

the patient will feel physically and mentally agitated, and all of this is a recipe for the "potential for violence, homicide and suicide."[50]

But these aren't the only possible side effects. Take a look at the package warning on a typically-prescribed antidepressant like Prozac: "ataxia [unbalanced walking]; bugogossia syndrome [smacking, spasmodic movements]; depression of the central nervous system; stimulation of the central nervous system; euphoria; hallucinations; hostility; fast movements; increased muscle tone; increased sensations; paranoid reaction; psychosis; dizziness."[51]

Her conclusion is that the incredible increase in use of antidepressants has "coincided" with the horrific school shootings that we have witnessed over the past two decades, yet all we as a nation have done in response is to focus on gun control.[52] I agree with Dr. Dolan's observations, and I also believe that it's time we shift the focus from gun control to an increased focus on controlling the psychiatric drugs responsible for altered judgment and reasoning, which lead to irrational and destructive behavior.

THE CASE OF CHRIS KYLE, THE AMERICAN SNIPER

The book/movie *The American Sniper* tells the story of a Navy SEAL war hero, Chris Kyle, who saved many lives over his four

---

50   The connection between violence, suicide, homicide, and antidepressants. (n.d.). Retrieved November 7, 2015, from http://www.encognitive.com/node/886
51   The connection between violence, suicide, homicide, and antidepressants. (n.d.). Retrieved November 7, 2015, from http://www.encognitive.com/node/886
52   http://www.encognitive.com/node/886

deployments into combat. He tried to help fellow veterans from the local Veterans Administration hospital overcome some of their emotional difficulties by taking them out to a local firing range.

One of these veterans, who was diagnosed with PTSD, killed Chris and his friend with a firearm while at the firing range. The week before this tragedy, I recall being on a radio show broadcast out of Texas where the shooting took place. The host of the show asked me if I felt our military veterans who had been diagnosed with PTSD should be allowed to purchase firearms. The host felt that these veterans should not be discriminated against and wanted to know if I agreed. Although he knew that I was not an anti-gun advocate, I surprised the host by stating that I do not believe anyone who is diagnosed with PTSD and is currently taking brain-altering psychiatric medications should be allowed to purchase a firearm.

I explained to the radio show host that it would be similar to allowing someone to drive a high-performance sports car on a racing track while drinking excessive amounts of alcohol. After putting it this way to the host, he understood my position. As a matter of fact, I stated to the host of the radio show that I would advocate for anyone on psychiatric medication(s) to be entered into a DOJ database that is available nationally to any store that sells firearms. Anyone on any type of psychiatric medication should not be allowed to own, or even shoot, a firearm until they are completely detoxified.

If someone is diagnosed with PTSD, there is a strong probability that a psychiatrist has prescribed him or her medication. This was the case with Chris Kyle's situation when he took Eddie Ray Routh to the firing range. Routh had a history of PTSD and mental health issues to the extent that he had been prescribed several psychiatric medications. It's very probable that Routh was experiencing an adverse reaction to the multiple medications. This may provide an explanation as to why Routh acted in such a violent manner for no apparent reason.

The award-winning journalist David Kupelian documented in his website article ("The Giant, Gaping Hole in Sandy Hook Reporting"), "it is indisputable that most perpetrators of school shootings and similar mass murders in our modern era were either on, or just recently coming off of, psychiatric medications."

Mr. Kupelian gave me permission to reprint his findings below, which include:

> Columbine mass-killer Eric Harris was taking Luvox – like Prozac, Paxil, Zoloft, Effexor and many others, a modern and widely prescribed type of antidepressant drug called selective serotonin reuptake inhibitors, or SSRIs. Harris and fellow student Dylan Klebold went on a hellish school shooting rampage in 1999 during which they killed 12 students and a teacher and wounded 24 others before turning their guns on themselves. Luvox manufacturer Solvay Pharmaceuticals concedes that during short-term controlled clinical trials, 4 percent of children and youth taking Luvox – that's 1 in 25 – developed mania, a danger-

ous and violence-prone mental derangement characterized by extreme excitement and delusion.

Patrick Purdy went on a schoolyard shooting rampage in Stockton, Calif., in 1989, which became the catalyst for the original legislative frenzy to ban "semiautomatic assault weapons" in California and the nation. The 25-year-old Purdy, who murdered five children and wounded 30, had been on Amitriptyline, an antidepressant, as well as the antipsychotic drug Thorazine.

Kip Kinkel, 15, murdered his parents in 1998 and the next day went to his school, Thurston High in Springfield, Ore., and opened fire on his classmates, killing two and wounding 22 others. He had been prescribed both Prozac and Ritalin.

In 1988, 31-year-old Laurie Dann went on a shooting rampage in a second-grade classroom in Winnetka, Ill., killing one child and wounding six. She had been taking the antidepressant Anafranil as well as Lithium, long used to treat mania.

In Paducah, Ky., in late 1997, 14-year-old Michael Carneal, son of a prominent attorney, traveled to Heath High School and started shooting students in a prayer meeting taking place in the school's lobby, killing three and leaving another paralyzed. Carneal reportedly was on Ritalin.

In 2005, 16-year-old Jeff Weise, living on Minnesota's Red Lake Indian Reservation, shot and killed nine people and wounded five others before killing himself. Weise had been taking Prozac.

In another famous case, 47-year-old Joseph T. Wesbecker, just a month after he began taking Prozac in 1989, shot 20 workers at Standard Gravure Corp. in Louisville, Ky., killing nine. Eli Lilly later settled a lawsuit brought by survivors.

Kurt Danysh, 18, shot his own father to death in 1996, a little more than two weeks after starting on Prozac. Danysh's description of own his mental-emotional state at the time of the murder is chilling: "I didn't realize I did it until after it was done," Danysh said. "This might sound weird, but it felt like I had no control of what I was doing, like I was left there just holding a gun."

John Hinckley, age 25, took four Valium two hours before shooting and almost killing President Ronald Reagan in 1981. In the assassination attempt, Hinckley also wounded press secretary James Brady, Secret Service agent Timothy McCarthy and policeman Thomas Delahanty.

Andrea Yates, in one of the most heartrending crimes in modern history, drowned all five of her children – aged 7 years down to 6 months – in a bathtub. Insisting inner voices commanded her to kill her children, she had become increasingly psychotic over the course of several years. At her 2006 murder re-trial (after a 2002 guilty verdict was overturned on appeal), Yates' longtime friend Debbie Holmes testified: "She asked me if I thought Satan could read her mind and if I believed in demon possession." And

Dr. George Ringholz, after evaluating Yates for two days, recounted an experience she had after the birth of her first child: "What she described was feeling a presence … Satan … telling her to take a knife and stab her son Noah," Ringholz said, adding that Yates' delusion at the time of the bathtub murders was not only that she had to kill her children to save them, but that Satan had entered her and that she had to be executed in order to kill Satan.

Yates had been taking the antidepressant Effexor. In November 2005, more than four years after Yates drowned her children, Effexor manufacturer Wyeth Pharmaceuticals quietly added "homicidal ideation" to the drug's list of "rare adverse events." The Medical Accountability Network, a private nonprofit focused on medical ethics issues, publicly criticized Wyeth, saying Effexor's "homicidal ideation" risk wasn't well publicized and that Wyeth failed to send letters to doctors or issue warning labels announcing the change.

And what exactly does "rare" mean in the phrase "rare adverse events"? The FDA defines it as occurring in less than one in 1,000 people. But since that same year 19.2 million prescriptions for Effexor were filled in the U.S., statistically that means thousands of Americans might experience "homicidal ideation" – murderous thoughts – as a result of taking just this one brand of antidepressant drug.

Effexor is Wyeth's best-selling drug, by the way, which in one recent year brought in over $3 billion in sales, accounting for almost a fifth of the company's annual revenues.

One more case is instructive, that of 12-year-old Christopher Pittman, who struggled in court to explain why he murdered his grandparents, who had provided the only love and stability he'd ever known in his turbulent life. "When I was lying in my bed that night," he testified, "I couldn't sleep because my voice in my head kept echoing through my mind telling me to kill them." Christopher had been angry with his grandfather, who had disciplined him earlier that day for hurting another student during a fight on the school bus. So later that night, he shot both of his grandparents in the head with a .410 shotgun as they slept and then burned down their South Carolina home, where he had lived with them." I got up, got the gun, and I went upstairs and I pulled the trigger," he recalled. "Through the whole thing, it was like watching your favorite TV show. You know what is going to happen, but you can't do anything to stop it." Pittman's lawyers would later argue that the boy had been a victim of "involuntary intoxication," since his doctors had him taking the antidepressants Paxil and Zoloft just prior to the murders.

Paxil's known "adverse drug reactions" – according to the drug's FDA-approved label – include "mania," "insomnia," "anxiety," "agitation," "confusion," "amnesia," "depression," "paranoid reaction," "psychosis," "hostility," "delirium," "hallucinations," "abnormal thinking," "depersonalization" and "lack of emotion," among others.

The preceding examples are only a few of the best-known offenders who had been taking prescribed psychiatric drugs before committing their violent crimes – there are many others.

Whether we like to admit it or not, it is undeniable that when certain people living on the edge of sanity take psychiatric medications, those drugs can – and occasionally do – push them over the edge into violent madness. Remember, every single SSRI antidepressant sold in the United States of America today, no matter what brand or manufacturer bears a "black box" FDA warning label – the government's most serious drug warning – of "increased risks of suicidal thinking and behavior, known as suicidality, in young adults ages 18 to 24." Common sense tells us that where there are suicidal thoughts – especially in a very, very angry person – homicidal thoughts may not be far behind. Indeed, the mass shooters we are describing often take their own lives when the police show up, having planned their suicide ahead of time.

So, what 'medication' was Lanza on?

The Sandy Hook school massacre, we are constantly reminded, was the "second-worst school shooting in U.S. history." Let's briefly revisit the worst, Virginia Tech, because it provides an important lesson for us. One would think, in light of the stunning correlation between psych meds and mass murders, that it would be considered critical to establish definitively whether the Virginia Tech murderer of 32 people, student Cho Seung-Hui, had been taking psychiatric drugs.

Yet, more than five years later, the answer to that question remains a mystery.

Even though initially the New York Times reported, "officials said prescription medications related to the treatment of psychological problems had been found among Mr. Cho's effects," and the killer's roommate, Joseph Aust, had told the Richmond Times-Dispatch that Cho's routine each morning had included taking prescription drugs, the state's toxicology report released two months later said "no prescription drugs or toxic substances were found in Cho Seung-Hui." Many of these meds have a half-life of 8 hours and are not detected in a normal toxicology corners report; therefore a history from witnesses is more accurate.

Perhaps so, but one of the most notoriously unstable and unpredictable times for users of SSRI antidepressants is the period shortly after they've stopped taking them, during which time the substance may not be detectable in the body.

What kind of meds might Cho have been taking – or recently have stopped taking? Curiously, despite an exhaustive investigation by the Commonwealth of Virginia, which disclosed that Cho had taken Paxil for a year in 1999, specifics on what meds he was taking prior to the Virginia Tech massacre have remained elusive. The final 20,000-word report manages to omit any conclusive information about the all-important issue of Cho's medications during the period of the mass shooting.

To add to the drama, it wasn't until two years after the state's in-depth report was issued that, as disclosed in an Aug. 19, 2009, ABC News report, some of Cho's long-missing mental health records were located: The records released today were discovered to be missing during a Virginia panel's August 2007 investigation four-and-a-half months after the massacre.

The notes were recovered last month from the home of Dr. Robert Miller, the former director of the counseling center, who says he inadvertently packed Cho's file into boxes of personal belongings when he left the center in February 2006. Until the July 2009 discovery of the documents, Miller said he had no idea he had the records. Miller has since been let go from the university.

Although Cho's newly discovered mental-health files reportedly revealed nothing further about his medications, the issues raised by the initial accounts – including the "officials" cited by the New York Times and the Richmond paper's eyewitness account of daily meds taking remain unaddressed to this day.

Some critics suggest these official omissions are motivated by a desire to protect the drug companies from ruinous product liability claims. Indeed, pharmaceutical manufacturers are nervous about lawsuits over the "rare adverse effects" of their mood-altering medications. To avoid costly settlements and public relations catastrophes such as when GlaxoSmithKline was ordered to pay $6.4 million to the family of 60-year-old Donald Schnell who murdered his wife, daughter and granddaughter in a fit of rage shortly after starting on Paxil – drug companies' legal teams have quietly and skillfully settled hundreds of cases out-of-court, shelling out hundreds of millions of dollars to plaintiffs. Pharmaceutical giant Eli Lilly fought scores of legal claims against Prozac in this way, settling for cash before the complaint could go to court while stipulating that the settlement remain secret and then claiming it had never lost a Prozac lawsuit.

All of which is, once again, to respectfully but urgently ask the question: When on earth are we going to find out if the perpetrator of the Sandy Hook school massacre, like so many other mass shooters, had been taking psychiatric drugs? In the end, it may well turn out that knowing what kinds of guns he used isn't nearly as important as what kind of drugs he used. That is, assuming we ever find out.[53]

End of Article

Other medical doctors have found equally disturbing symptoms and syndromes that can result when people take certain drugs, especially when these drugs are taken for PTSD or other neurological conditions. In fact, in *The Attorney's Guide to Defending Veterans in Criminal Court,* Dr. Peter Breggin, MD, wrote a chapter titled, "Traumatic Brain Injury (TBI), Posttraumatic Stress Disorder (PTSD) and Antidepressant Drugs: A Per-

---

53   Kupelian, D. (2013, January 6). The giant, gaping hole in Sandy Hook reporting. Retrieved November 8, 2015, from http://www.wnd.com/2013/01/the-giant-gaping-hole-in-sandy-hook-reporting/. Reprinted with permission.

fect Storm for Causing Abnormal Mental States and Behavior."
In this chapter, he shares many interesting conclusions. I have
reprinted Dr. Breggin's summary below with his permission:

(1) Traumatic Brain Injury (TBI) and Posttraumatic
Stress Disorder (PTSD) display many similar symptoms,
such as insomnia, hypersensitivity, anxiety, agitation, irritability, and a potentially dangerous loss of impulse control, leading to violence and suicide. This is especially true
during the first several weeks or months of PTSD and/or
TBL Acute TBI and PTSD, thus, can partially mimic and
worsen each other.

(2) If TBI and/or PTSD remain inadequately treated
over a period of months and years, both are likely to cause
similar clinical symptoms of cognitive impairment, apathy
or indifference, social withdrawal, fatigue, depression and
suicidality, emotional instability or lability, and a general
limitation on the quality of life. In the case of TBl, this syndrome is caused by Chronic Brain Impairment (CBI); but
in the case of PTSD it is caused by chronic psychological
stress. Chronic TBI and PTSD thus can mimic and can
worsen each other.

(3). Antidepressants, stimulants, benzodiazepines,
some mood stabilizers, antipsychotic drugs (akathisia) and
other psychiatric drugs can produce insomnia, anxiety,
irritability, impulsivity, disinhibition, emotional instability,
depression, suicide, violence and mania. This is especially
likely to happen within several weeks or months of the start

of medication, during medication changes, and during medication adjustments up or down in dose. Acute treatment with psychiatric drugs, thus, can mimic and worsen TBI and PTSD.

(4) If antidepressants or any other psychiatric drugs are given longer-term (months or years), they tend to produce Chronic Brain Impairment (CBI) similar or nearly identical to the trauma-induced CBL and also similar to the chronic psychological symptoms of PTSD. Chronic exposure to any psychiatric drug, thus, can mimic and worsen TBI and PTSD.

(5) TBI, PTSD, and antidepressant drugs, separately and together, can greatly compromise cognitive abilities, emotional stability, self-insight, and concern for self. They also cause anosognosia or lack of awareness of their deficits. In the legal arena, this is important not only in regard to causing suicide, violence and crime, it is also important in regard to competency to make judgments during the legal proceedings and to properly assist counsel.

(6) Since all psychiatric drugs can cause medication spellbinding and chronic brain impairment (CBI), they can contribute to or cause abnormal mental and behavioral states related to suicide, violence, and criminal activity; and they can compromise judgment and competence during legal proceedings. The risk is increased when the drugs are combined with PTSD and/or TBI.

(7) Because psychiatric drugs, TBI, and PTSD produce overlapping symptoms during both the acute and the chronic phases, prescribers and other clinicians are likely to believe the patient's TBI and/or PTSD are getting worse, when in fact the patient is being made worse by exposure to the psychiatric drugs. This can lead to a mistaken increase in psychiatric drug exposure, creating a vicious cycle in which the patient is exposed to more of the offending medication, with the result of a much worsened condition.

(8) Antidepressants and other psychiatric drugs are almost always poor choices for the treatment of PTSD or TBI, and should never be relied upon as exclusive treatments. Some healthcare providers have found that short-term, low dose medications are useful, along with psychotherapeutic approaches; but even this should be done with caution and restraint by experienced clinicians. Routine clinical doses and/or long-term exposure to psychiatric drugs, as well as polydrug exposure, will do far more harm than good to individuals suffering from TBI or PTSD.

(9) As I describe in Psychiatric Drug Withdrawal (2013), removal from psychiatric drugs must be done carefully and slowly with experienced clinical supervision in a collaborative team effort involving the prescriber, the therapist, the patient and the family. Withdrawing patients from psychiatric drugs will often produce a dramatic improvement in TBI and PTSD, as well as in drug-induced CBI.

(10) Although not the focus of this chapter, many empathic approaches are available for the treatment of TBI and PTSD. All require a caring, supportive therapeutic relationship that optimally involves the family as well. For more information on empathic approaches, please see the Center for the Study of Empathic Therapy's website at www.empathictherapy.org.[54]

End of article

With all of the above in mind, it's easy to see that adverse effects of psychiatric drugs are being ignored as a contributing cause to suicide.

The findings of a military medical school study in *Health Day News* reported that:

Among U.S. Army personnel, enlisted soldiers on their first tour of duty appear to be most at risk for attempted suicide ... Concerned by a spike in suicides and suicide attempts in the Army during the Iraq and Afghanistan wars, researchers set out to identify key risks for suicide attempts between 2004 and 2009 ... [and they found that] Those who were female, younger, early in their career, with a recent mental health problem, and never or previously deployed were at greatest risk.[55]

---

54   Hunter, B. (2014). TBI, PTSD, and Psychiatric Drugs: A Perfect Storm for Causing Abnormal Mental States and Aberrant Behavior. In *The attorney's guide to defending veterans in criminal court*. Minneapolis, MN: Veterans Defense Project.
55   Mozes, A. (2015, July 9). Newly Enlisted Army Soldiers at Risk of Attempted Suicide: Study. Retrieved November 14, 2015, from http://consumer.healthday.com/general-health-information-16/military-health-news-763/investigation-identifies-main-suicide-risk-factors-among-u-s-Army-soldiers-701176.html

The study avoided stating whether the suicide victims with recent mental health issues were on psychiatric medications. If they were identified as having a recent mental health issue, the probability is high they were prescribed at least one psychiatric medication with a black box warning indicating suicidal ideation as a side effect.

CHAPTER 4

PSYCHIATRIC MEDICATION AND RELATIONSHIP TO DEAD-IN-BED SYNDROME & TRAUMATIC BRAIN INJURY

In February of 2014, I was invited to attend the Citizens Commission on Human Rights International (CCHR) awards gala, held in Los Angeles, California. This is a once-a-year event where a few individuals working in the fields of mental health human rights are recognized. It was an honor for me to be one of the four individuals being recognized for their work in the field of mental health. Most of all, I was impressed with the other three individuals receiving awards.

One award was given to Pat Mena, who lost a son to dead-in-bed syndrome. Pat wrote a book (*You'll Be Fine, Darling: Struggling with PTSD after the Trauma of War*) explaining what happened to her airman son Anthony when he returned from combat. He was diagnosed with PTSD and over an extended period of time was given multiple psychiatric medications. Pat explained what a good person he was and what an outstanding soldier he turned out to be. Part of being an outstanding soldier and becoming a non-commissioned officer (NCO) required him to follow orders. This positive trait extended to following his doctor's orders in taking his multiple psychiatric medications.

One day, when Pat called her son to see how he was doing, there was no answer. She later discovered that her son had died in his sleep. The coroner's report listed the cause of death as an adverse toxic reaction to the combination of psychiatric medications he was taking. When Pat later tried to seek justice, she could not find an attorney who would take the case on a contingency basis. Pat and her husband could not afford to hire an attorney. Her alternative was to make people aware of what not only happened to her son Anthony, but what has been and continues to happen to other veterans by writing a book about their experience.

Pat Mena's story is not an isolated case. Although there have been numerous articles and papers written on the connection between psychiatric cocktails and sudden death, not much has been done by our government, or the medical profession, to curb this continuing problem.

Mikal Vega, another human rights awardee and a former Navy SEAL, received an award for programs he developed in Los Angeles for veterans. His own experience of returning home from combat and being heavily medicated to the point of feeling like he was going to die was quite shocking. According to Mikal, being on multiple tours of combat and being injured while in combat was not as life threatening as the multiple psychiatric medications he was prescribed when he came home. He was very close to experiencing the ultimate adverse effects of these medications—sudden death or suicide. Due to his inner strength and determination, he was able to get off the psychiatric medications and learn integrative treatment modalities to overcome his PTS. His experience led him to develop an integrative treatment program for other veterans where psychiatric medications are not prescribed.

Another award went to attorney Allison Folmar, who was instrumental in saving a young child from potential deadly psychiatric medications. Her work as an attorney representing this child and her mother actually changed laws for treating children without parental consent in the state and city where the case was heard.

The overall CCHR yearly gala and awards ceremony was inspiring; 1000 people attended from countries around the world. It reminds me of Albert Einstein's quote, "The world is a dangerous place to live; not because of the people who are evil, but because of the people who don't do anything about it."[56] The

---

56   lbert Einstein quotes. (n.d.). Retrieved November 1, 2015, from http://www.brainyquote.com/quotes/quotes/a/alberteins143096.html

members of CCHR are apparently doing something about the evils of mental health abuses on an international scale.

Prior to hearing about Pat Mena's son's sudden death, one of the first major stories that I became aware of on the subject of veterans dying in their sleep was written by the Charleston Gazette's staff writer, Julie Robinson. She wrote about the death of Marine veteran Andrew White, who died in his sleep while taking Seroquel (an antipsychotic drug) for PTSD.

"Stan White, father of soldier Andrew White, has become an advocate for families of returning veterans with post-traumatic stress disorder. During his son's struggle with the disorder and since his death, White has tracked similar cases and knows of about eight in the tri-state area of Kentucky, Ohio and West Virginia."[57]

Meanwhile, Christopher Byron states in his article, "The Deadliest Prescription Drug in America" that "reports began to surface of soldiers returning from Iraq with post-traumatic stress disorder who were dying in their sleep, the victims of a psych-med cocktail of Klonopin, Paxil (an antidepressant), and Seroquel (an antipsychotic) that is routinely prescribed by VA hospitals."[58]

Some doctors refuse to maintain the status quo and leave. For example, Dr. Grace Jackson "resigned her commission ... 'because

---

57 Are PTSD-Medicated Veterans Dying in Sleep -- or Committing Suicide? (2008, June 7). Retrieved November 1, 2015, from http://ptsdcombat.blogspot.com/2008/06/are-ptsd-medicated-veterans-dying-in.html
58 Byron, C. (2015, February 10). The Deadliest Prescription Drug in America? Retrieved November 1, 2015, from http://www.alternet.org/drugs/deadliest-prescription-drug-america

[she] did not want to be a pill pusher.'"[59] According to Jackson, even though the Army has acknowledged "problems associated with at least one class of psychiatric medication … [they do] not address problems with other classes of prescription drugs."[60]

"The Army also has ignored the role antipsychotic drugs play in the "sudden deaths" of troops diagnosed with traumatic brain injury due to undiagnosed endocrine abnormalities," according to Jackson.[61] "The use of antipsychotic drugs to treat troops with TBI can cause changes in growth and thyroid hormones, which can in turn trigger a variety of cardiac-related events that could result in sudden deaths. … Though the Army has adopted a new policy on the use of benzodiazepines, the Defense Department overall is still wedded to a policy of using drugs to treat mental problems even when scientific evidence demonstrates poor risk-benefit ratios.

"The Army policy memo encouraged clinicians to look beyond drugs to treat PTSD and suggested a range of alternative therapies, including yoga, biofeedback, acupuncture and massage."[62]

But Andrew White isn't the only death under these circumstances. In fact, neurologist Dr. Fred Baughman has discovered that there are many more veterans, such as twenty-nine year old

---

59   Brewing, B. (2012, April 25). Army warns doctors against using certain drugs in PTSD treatment. Retrieved November 1, 2015, from http://www.nextgov.com/defense/2012/04/broken-warriors-test/55389/
60   Brewing, B. (2012, April 25). Army warns doctors against using certain drugs in PTSD treatment. Retrieved November 1, 2015, from http://www.nextgov.com/defense/2012/04/broken-warriors-test/55389/
61   Brewing, B. (2012, April 25). Army warns doctors against using certain drugs in PTSD treatment. Retrieved November 1, 2015, from http://www.nextgov.com/defense/2012/04/broken-warriors-test/55389/
62   http://veteransforcommonsense.org/2012/04/27/Army-warns-doctors-against-using-certain-drugs-in-ptsd-treatment/

Eric Layne, twenty-two-year-old Derek Johnson, and Nicholas Endicott—who have died while taking drugs to treat PTSD (but were considered "normal" in all other respects).[63] Dr. Baughman strongly suspects that over 400 soldiers died of sudden death causes including military veterans Andrew White, Eric Layne, Nicholas Endicott, and Derek Johnson and believes that they were not suicidal or the victims of overdoses as is often the reason given by the military. Instead, Dr. Baughman believes that cocktails of prescription drugs are to blame.[64] Other doctors have concurred: "antidepressants also increase the rate of sudden cardiac deaths."[65]

Furthermore, in a literature review covering the years 2000-2007, entitled "Sudden Cardiac Death Secondary to Antidepressant and Antipsychotic Drugs," Dr. Serge Sicouri and Dr. Charles Antzelevitch conclude: (1) "A number of antipsychotic and antidepressant drugs can increase the risk of ventricular arrhythmias and sudden cardiac death (2) Antipsychotics can increase cardiac risk even at low doses whereas antidepressants do it generally at high doses or in the setting of drug combinations, and (3) These observations call for an ECG at baseline and after drug administration."[66]

63   Robinson, J. (2012, May 28). Couple continues battle after soldier son's PTSD treatment-related death. Retrieved November 1, 2015, from http://www.wvgazettemail.com/News/201205280085

64   Tighman, A. (2010, May 26). Psych Drugs Killing U.S. Military Vets In Their Sleep. Retrieved November 1, 2015, from http://www.rense.com/general90/sleep.htm

65   Tighman, A. (2010, May 26). Psych Drugs Killing U.S. Military Vets In Their Sleep. Retrieved November 1, 2015, from http://www.rense.com/general90/sleep.htm

66   Sicouri, S., & Antzelevitch, C. (n.d.). Sudden cardiac death secondary to antidepressant and antipsychotic drugs. Retrieved November 21, 2015, from http://www.ncbi.nlm.nih.gov/pmc/articles/PMC2365731/

Perhaps most disturbing is the information regarding the suspicious death of veteran Ryan Alderman: "Pfc. Ryan Alderman was also on a never-justifiable cocktail of antipsychotic and antidepressant drugs when he was found dead in his barracks at Ft. Carson, Colo. Sudden cardiac death was confirmed by EKG by emergency medical technicians at the scene, but reclassified as "suicide." Why? By whom?"[67]

However, the above information hasn't translated into preventive monitoring, as seen in a report from the Inspector General for Veterans Affairs. "(Report No. 08-01377-185): 'Although antipsychotic medications have been identified as possible causes of cardiac rhythm disturbances, a 2001 review... found no association with olanzapine (Zyprexa), quetiapine (Seroquel), or risperidone (Risperdal) and Torsades de Pointes (a fatal heart rhythm) or sudden death. We are unaware of any clinical practice guidelines recommending baseline or periodic electrocardiogram monitoring in young, healthy patients on quetiapine (Seroquel)."[68]

VETERANS WITH TBI

Research at Johns Hopkins revealed "they may have found the signature of 'shell shock' - a problem that has afflicted many sol-

---

67   Baughman, F. (n.d.). Fred A. Baughman Jr., MD Announces: Vets' Deaths Are Not Suicides or 'Overdoses' but Sudden Cardiac Deaths Due to Prescription Antipsychotics and Antidepressants. Retrieved November 1, 2015, from
68   http://www.prnewswire.com/news-releases/fred-a-baughman-jr-md-announces-vets-deaths-are-not-suicides-or-overdoses-but-sudden-cardiac-deaths-due-to-prescription-antipsychotics-and-antidepressants-94730024.html

diers since World War One warfare."[69] Apparently, the force from an IED (improvised explosive devices) is different from external trauma to the head; that's because the blast generates vibrations that originate in the chest and then affect the frontal lobe of the brain. The frontal lobe is responsible for "executive functions … functions that allow you to put your life together, organize, plan ahead, [and] understand abstract. And you can imagine this [type of brain trauma] can make your life difficult."[70]

BRAIN TRAUMA AND PTSD

In 2014, I was reading a San Diego paper about research that was being conducted by a psychiatrist at the University of California San Diego. Her conclusion was that individuals experiencing a traumatic brain injury often wound up with related PTSD. In the words of American philosopher Josh Billings, "Common sense is instinct and enough of it is genius."[71]

Most people in the mental health profession would understand that a TBI alone would most likely cause a normal PTS reaction. So if you have a TBI resultant from combat, not only would you have a normal reaction to this very abnormal injury, but you would experience the usual PTS reaction from the battlefield as well.

---

69   Kitchener, J. (2015, August 13). Hidden damage revealed in veterans' brains from IED blasts. Retrieved November 14, 2015, from http://www.reuters.com/article/2015/08/13/us-usa-veterans-brains-idU.S.KCN0QI21I20150813#WmOj9Et3R8xbR6b3.97
70   Kitchener, J. (2015, August 13). Hidden damage revealed in veterans' brains from IED blasts. Retrieved November 14, 2015, from http://www.reuters.com/article/2015/08/13/us-usa-veterans-brains-idU.S.KCN0QI21I20150813#WmOj9Et3R8xbR6b3.97
71   http://www.brainyquote.com/quotes/quotes/j/joshbillin136485.html

When discussing TBI, it is not uncommon to look at chronic traumatic encephalopathy (CTE). This is due to the extensive media attention on head injuries experienced by athletes, specifically in the National Football League (NFL). The movie titled *Concussion* (released 12/25/15) is the story of how pathologist Bennet Omalu, MD discovered CTE in deceased NFL football players. I strongly recommend that anyone interested in this subject view this movie.

Encephalopathy by itself means a disease of, malfunction of, or damage to the brain, which can result in an altered mental state or physical changes to a person. Since the term encephalopathy is very broad, it is usually preceded by the term that specifically identifies the type of encephalopathy being described. For instance, damage to the brain can be caused by liver disease (hepatic encephalopathy), oxygen deprivation (anoxic encephalopathy), and in the case of multiple impacts to the head, the identifying diagnosis would be chronic traumatic encephalopathy.[72]

In its early stages, symptoms of CTE include "memory problems, disorientation, and difficulty concentrating ... [but as the disease] progresses, people begin to show poor judgment, erratic behavior, significant memory loss and some degree of Parkinson's disease." This disease "is also commonly associated with psychological problems like depression, agitation, aggression and violence, loss of inhibitions, drug and alcohol abuse and suicide."[73]

---

72   http://www.medicinenet.com/script/main/art.asp?articlekey=101343
73   Athletes' Dementia: Understanding Chronic Traumatic Encephalopathy. (n.d.). Retrieved November 1, 2015, from http://www.healthafter50.com/alerts/memory/athlete-dementia_3871-1.html

In 2014, I had an opportunity to speak with Willie James Buchanon, a former cornerback for the Green Bay Packers and San Diego Chargers. I met Willie at a wellness conference and discussed with him the need for his association to be aware of the significant adverse effects that a football player with potential CTE may experience when taking psychiatric medications.

When talking with Willie, I explained that I had been on a local San Diego sports radio show discussing the suicide death of Junior Seau, a Hall of Fame linebacker who lived in San Diego. The sports show that I appeared on aired shortly after Junior's death. I remember stating to the sports announcer that I felt Junior experienced CTE from playing years of football. The host of the show stated that there was no autopsy at that point in time and asked how I knew this. I explained that I strongly felt all football players, based on the nature of the sport, have experienced CTE to varying degrees. My comment at the time was based on my background of 48 years in the mental health field and experience working with all types of impairments including TBI. The following article which appeared in USA Today on 4-22-15 also supports my supposition; "Judge Approves Potential $1 Billion Settlement To Resolve NFL Concussion Lawsuit," which reported that 6000 retired NFL players will receive an average of $190K for concussion injuries.[74] Approximately one year after my first interview, I was invited back on the show to discuss the autopsy results, which showed that Junior did in fact have CTE.

---

74 (http://www.usatoday.com/story/sports/nfl/2015/04/22/nfl-concussion-lawsuit-settle-ment-judge-1-billion/26192827/).

I explained on the second radio show that adverse effects of psychiatric medication cocktails for TBI/CTE are more likely to appear and be even more severe when a person is also being prescribed potent pain relievers such as codeine, hydrocodone, Demerol, morphine, and/or oxycodone, which is not uncommon for football players and combat veterans.

Since anyone with a TBI or CTE has an increased risk of suicide—four times more than someone without this injury—combining narcotic pain relievers with brain-altering psychiatric medications sets up a perfect storm for sudden death, suicide, and other physical and psychological reactions.

After viewing the movie *Concussion*, I noticed that although mention was made to the deceased players using medication for pain relief, as well as psychiatric medications, there was no direct reference to these medications contributing to the actual behavior of the players being discussed. Therefore, I feel strongly that anyone having potential CTE or TBI should be aware that the first black box warning on most psychiatric medications is suicide. As this book states, there are multiple integrative treatment modalities that can be utilized for what is a very physical (not psychiatric) impairment of CTE or TBI.

Concussion also neglects to explore the relationship between psychiatric medication and dangerous physical side effects. For example, there is a scene in which a football player (Webster), who is later diagnosed post-mortem with CTE, was given an injection of Haldol (also known as Haloperidol) after he visits the NFL team physician in a very agitated state (which is not uncommon with a brain injury). Soon after, Webster has a heart attack and dies.

"Haloperidol, is also commonly used, both intramuscularly and intravenously, to control agitated patients in the emergency room. In September 2007, the FDA released a warning that torsades de pointes and QT prolongation (Heart rhythm) might occur in patients receiving haloperidol, particularly when the drug is administered intravenously or at doses higher than recommended. The FDA notes that haloperidol is not approved for intravenous use". This information can be seen in the Summary and Comment of the 10/12/07 issue of Emergency Medicine titled "FDA Warning: Haloperidol Joins Droperidol" by Diane M. Birnbaumer, MD, FACEP.[75]

Also an article in the Journal Of Hospital Medicine in 2010; 5(4): E8-E16 (PubMed: 20394022) titled, "The FDA extended warning for intravenous haloperidol and torsades de pointes: how should institutions respond" reveals some patients experiencing sudden cardiac arrest after given IV haloperidol, as well as other potential risk factors.[76]

The movie suggests that the football player had CTE but died from heart failure; the injection of Haldol was never addressed.

---

75   http://www.jwatch.org/em200710120000001/2007/10/12/fda-warning-haloperi-
     dol-joins-droperidol
76   www.ncbi.nlm.nih.gov/pubmedhealth/PMHOO30925/

CHAPTER 5

CONGRESSIONAL HEARINGS TESTIMONY REGARDING SUICIDES AND PSYCHIATRIC MEDICATIONS IN THE MILITARY

On June 5, 2015, I received an e-mail regarding The House Committee on Veterans Affairs (HVAC) Media Advisory, which was for immediate release on June 5, 2015. The title on the advisory was: "HVAC to Examine Prescription Mismanagement and the Risk of Veteran Suicide."

The previous congressional hearings I initiated and rendered testimony for regarding the relationship of psychiatric medications and suicide in the military took place on February 24, 2010 and addressed this same issue. The hearings then were entitled "Exploring the Relationship Between Medication and Veteran Suicide." It took the House Committee on Veterans' Affairs over five years to get formally back to this subject. After the initial hearings in 2010, it did not appear to me that the committee took the matter very seriously since I observed no direct follow-up. However, Congress is back to the subject and hopefully this time some positive, observable action will result in helping save our veterans' lives. Their most recent email news release stated:

"WASHINGTON, DC — On Wednesday, June 10, 2015 at 10:30 a.m. in room 334 of the Cannon House Office Building, the House Committee on Veterans Affairs Subcommittee on Oversight & Investigations will hold a hearing to examine prescription mismanagement and the risk of veteran suicide."

Further stated on the same email news release was:

> A series of investigations at the Tomah VAMC revealed skyrocketing opiate prescriptions and found 33 unexpected deaths at the facility veterans dubbed "candy land." Earlier this week, a hidden camera video released by Project Veritas shows VA officials admitting problems with over-prescribing dangerous medications, leading to veterans developing addictions. The VA VISN with the lowest rate of opiate prescriptions in the country uses a novel solution—diagnose first. The subcommittee is investigating the VA's increased opiate use in connection to incidents of assaults, suicide, and

murder among veterans, the lack of monitoring and follow up for veterans prescribed medications as treatment for various mental health issues, and the inconsistent and inaccurate data accumulated by VA regarding the diagnoses of veterans with mental disorders and their subsequent suicides. This hearing will look into how the VA's over reliance on medication may be harming veterans and increasing the risk of suicide.[77]

After calling and learning that the HVAC has been investigating the VA for years, my sentiment on no action by them softened. I submitted questions to the committee for the hearings, of which one was asked. After viewing the hour- and-a-half long hearings of the House of Representatives, Veterans Affairs Committee Hearings, I was both frustrated and angered by the responses from staff representing the Veterans Administration. I had intended to write a summary impression immediately after the hearings but due to my own frustration, I felt I needed to clear my mind regarding how the VA staff avoided answering direct questions from the committee. What I did is follow one of my own recommendations in my book to reduce stress—take a yoga class.

One of the classic statements that went through my mind in the middle of the yoga class was that if you don't challenge an organization's perceptions, those perceptions eventually become reality and policy. I was pleased to see members of the

---

77 House Committee on Veterans Affairs. (2015). HVAC to Examine Prescription Mismanagement and the Risk of Veteran Suicide [Press release]. Print.

congressional committee challenging the VA staff's policies and insisting on answers to very specific, troubling questions regarding our veteran's care. As a clinical psychologist with extensive experience in program development and management, I have always looked at how people communicate, both verbally and nonverbally. I recall one of my previous professors stating that psychologists are trained observers.

It was obvious to me that the Congressional Veterans Affairs Committee was extremely concerned about the well-being of our soldiers. Their body language, tone, and what they said showed a strong sense of caring for our veterans. Their sincerity in wanting to help was forthcoming throughout the hour and a half meeting. They identified areas that needed to be improved and also discussed some of the positive programs that they had observed at the VA. They tried to make it clear that their purpose was to work with the VA staff to help improve services for our veterans.

The VA, on the other hand, appeared to be practicing what the military calls SERE: survival, evasion, resistance, and escape. My perception was that they did not provide answers in a short and concise manner. They resisted requests made by congressmen for information to the point where congressional staff explained to them that Congress represents the people of the United States and has every right to receive information from the VA on their services. It was surprising to me that this had to be explained to the chief staff member representing the Veterans Administration.

Although the VA staff stated that they appreciated the help from the congressional committee, my observation was that their body language and tone was not consistent with sincerity. Instead of appreciating the extensive research done by the congressional committee in order to help create better programs, there was a sense of regret that this information was revealed. There were many questions asked by the committee that the VA staff did not have answers for; the VA stated that they would have to get back to them with answers.

Hopefully the many unanswered questions will be addressed at the next hearing. Also, the congressional committee will be submitting many more questions between now and the next meeting. Since these hearings only lasted for one and a half hours, it was very difficult to accomplish all that is necessary to improve services at the VA. In the future, meetings of this nature would realistically need to take days, instead of hours, to be successful. Some, but not all, of the questions that I recall being asked were:

1. Currently, how many staff vacancies exist within the Veterans Administration?

2. Since there were 63 behavioral health autopsy reports initiated by the VA, why were two-thirds not complete?

3. Why are there patterns of the Veterans Administration non-compliance with standards of excellence?

4. Why is it that the Veterans Administration reports one-half of all suicides receiving VA services involve

medication overdoses? Why aren't these medications more closely monitored?

5. Why is it that the veterans' suicide hotline at the VA does not go directly to a counselor but takes various extension numbers before a person can finally get to speak with someone?

6. Why are one in three veterans seen at the VA prescribed psychiatric medications?

7. Why are one-third of all veterans applying for mental health services in El Paso VA not seen at all (asked by the congressman from Texas)?

8. Why is it that over the past 7 years, there has been a 74% increase in the VA's budget with no real significant improvements in services being provided in regards to mental health issues?

9. Why does it appear that there is no accountability for the VA's poor performance in providing services and treatments specific to mental health issues?

10. Why has the VA not provided the written materials requested by this congressional committee?

11. How many physiatrists does the Veterans Administration employ nationally (asked by the chairman of the Veterans Affairs committee)?

My Overall Recommendations:

Do not allow the VA four to six months to set up a direct suicide prevention line that will immediately be answered by a counselor. This line could be set up within a week. At a rate of twenty-two veteran suicides a day, I was startled that the chief representative from the VA would be so lackadaisical about the urgency of setting up a suicide prevention immediate answer hotline.

Most of the questions regarding medication and suicide dealt with narcotics for pain. There was some mention of brain-altering psychiatric medications but not significantly so. The next meeting with the VA representatives should stress, along with narcotic medications, the serious adverse effects of psychiatric medications.

Future questions I suggest that the VA staff be asked include:

1. A study in the January 2009 issue of the New England Journal of Medicine found the rate of sudden cardiac death doubled for those taking atypical antipsychotic drugs. What investigations have and does the VA take into "sudden deaths" or apparent inexplicable deaths when antipsychotics alone or in combination with other psychotropic and/or opiates have been prescribed?

2. What due diligence has the VA taken to ensure that in each of these sudden deaths, no malpractice or negligence has occurred?

3. Outside the military, doctors have been convicted of manslaughter and culpable negligence for prescribing

addictive or dangerous cocktails of medicines. What, if any, action has the VA taken to ensure accountability for negligent prescribing?

4. Is the VA aware of the off-label prescribing report that the Office of Defense Research and Engineering (ODDR&E) commissioned from the Mitre Corporation? What will the VA do to reduce off-label prescribing of psychotropic drug use, especially antipsychotics being prescribed off-label, among vets?

5. What policy does the VA have regarding conflicts of interests between their prescribing physicians and pharmaceutical companies? Is it aware of any conflicts of interest regarding specific doctors and, if so, what monitoring does it conduct to ensure that unsafe prescription trends—potentially influenced by such conflict—are not occurring (which could put vets at risk)?

6. How does the VA monitor the effectiveness of its mental health programs to ensure accountability for both expenditures and, more importantly, the positive outcome of treated vets?

7. The Food & Drug Administration has detailed recommendations on antidepressant labels advising patients, as well as third parties such as caretakers and family, to monitor the patient for possible signs of suicidality upon starting the drug or changing dosage and advising immediate reference to a health care provider if any

of those signs appear. Are VA doctors doing that? If not, why not?

MY TESTIMONY FOR THE VETERANS' AFFAIRS COMMITTEE OF THE HOUSE OF REPRESENTATIVES ON FEBRUARY 24, 2010

These hearings in Congress were the result of the findings at the yearly International Military and Civilian Combat Stress Conference. Since this conference is the longest running conference of its type in the world (twenty-two years and counting) and is considered by many to be the gold standard, many elected officials and military dignitaries have quite often been in attendance. During one such occasion, the congressman who was the chairman of the Veterans' Affairs Committee was in attendance. His attendance was quite impressive since it was the second time he attended the conference. Not only did he speak at the conference but also he stayed to listen to several of the presenters, have lunch with conference participants, and listen to their concerns.

For about one year I communicated with this congressman, requesting that he initiate congressional hearings to look at the relationship between adverse effects of psychiatric medications and resultant suicides by our veterans. Since the rate of veteran suicide was extremely high, averaging twenty-two a day, he was receptive to initiating the requested hearings. Active duty suicides were also increasing dramatically and, at times, more active duty military personnel were dying from suicide than were being killed in combat.

The following is my testimony for the 2010 Congressional hearings:

Submissions for the Record

Bart P. Billings, PhD, Carlsbad, CA (Psychologist and Author)

February 24, 2010

10:00AM Room 334 Cannon House Office Building

Hearings » Exploring the Relationship between Medication and Veteran Suicide

Statement of Bart P. Billings, PhD Carlsbad, CA (Psychologist and Author)

I. Role of Psychiatric Medications in Suicide:

If you were the parent of a son or daughter serving in the military, would you want your child being prescribed medication, on the battlefield or off, which contained a black-box warning that states the following:

> Suicidality and Antidepressant Drugs. Antidepressants increased the risk compared to placebo of suicidal thinking and behavior (suicidality) in children, adolescents, and young adults in short-term studies of major depressive disorder (MDD) and other psychiatric disorders. Anyone considering the use of (name of drug) or any other antidepressant

in a child, adolescent, or young adult must balance this risk with the clinical need. A medication guide appears at the end of the label. The prescriber or health professional should instruct patients, their families, and their caregivers to read the medication guide and should assist them in understanding its contents.

The medication guide also gives specific guidance about identifying danger signs:

Call a health care provider right away if you or your family member has any of the following symptoms especially if they are new, worse, or worry you:

(1)   Thoughts about suicide or dying

(2)   Attempts to commit suicide

(3)   New or worsening depression

(4)   New or worsening anxiety

(5)   Feeling very agitated or restless

(6)   Panic attacks

(7)   Trouble sleeping (insomnia)

(8)   New or worsening irritability

(9)   Acting aggressive, being angry, or violent

(10)   Acting on dangerous impulses

(11)   An extreme increase in activity and talking (mania)

(12)   Other unusual changes in behavior or mood

Identical or nearly identical warnings and information can be found in all antidepressants labels. The strongest warning pertains to children and young adults up to age 24, which includes many young military personnel.

From 2002 through 2008, there has been nearly a doubling of psychiatric medications prescribed to our military personnel and their families. At the same time, there has been a surge in the number of suicides among service members and their family members that appears to correlate directly with the increase use of psychiatric medication.

Stop and think about the fact that military personnel, who carry a weapon 24 hours a day, seven days a week, for a year deployment, can be given a medication that has a black box warning, indicating a potential side effect can be suicide as well as aggressive, angry and violent behavior that can lead to homicide. If a medical practitioner prescribed this type of medication in the civilian community, to a patient who constantly carried a loaded weapon (had a permit to do so) and had extensive training on how to use this weapon, they could likely be charged with mal-practice and possibly lose their license to practice medicine. If there was a suicide or homicide by this patient, directly related to this prescription, then the practitioner could be criminally charged.

When discussing this issue with several civilian private practice physicians, they stated that they would not prescribe psychiatric medications to this type of patient but would refer the patient for counseling. This is not the case with many Veterans

Administration (VA) psychiatrists, who in most cases prescribe psychiatric medications to the veterans they treat.

In 2008, the New York Times reported Dr. Ira Katz, head of mental health services in the VA wrote an email to his staff stating: The VA should be quiet about the rate of suicide attempts with veterans receiving VA services. It should be noted that about 1000 suicide attempts a month were reported in veterans seen at VA facilities. Again, one must look at the relationship between extensive numbers of psychiatric medication being prescribed at the VA and the large number of suicides and attempted suicides by veterans receiving services at the VA.

In 2007, a reporter, Rick Rogers from the San Diego Union Tribune, published a story stating that more Marines died at Camp Pendleton from suicide, homicide and motorcycle accidents (34 percent increase in motorcycle deaths between 2007 and 2008) than Marines deployed from Camp Pendleton who died in combat.

This same reporter reported that Marines and other military personnel were being sent into combat while on psychiatric medication. He was one of the first reporters in the country to report on this policy, developed by the chief psychiatrist's in all military services.

The questions that need to be asked:

How can medical practitioners in the military and the VA get away with what, in the civilian community, could be considered mal-practice and in certain cases criminal?

Why are military mental health psychiatrists or their disciples, who initially recommended the use of these types of medication to their mental health subordinates, who are located on the battlefield, still in positions of leadership and funded, with the responsibility to explain the causes of continued escalation of suicides in the military?

Why hasn't there been a change in mental health leadership who has consistently failed to stop the drastic increase in suicides and homicides in the military?

Why haven't there been widely published post mortem reports on all suicides and homicides, both on the battlefield and at home, clearly identifying if the victim was on psychiatric medications?

Does anyone believe that military mental health staff who advocated initially using psychiatric medication, will ever do research that demonstrates that the same medications they recommended be used on our military personnel has direct side effects that can lead to suicide and homicide?

Hopefully some, if not all of these questions can be answered in testimony provided at these congressional hearings. I don't believe the current increase in suicides and homicides in the military is a coincidence, based on my personal observations, as well as other professionals' observations and writings on the subject. A recent text, "Medication Madness" written by a world renowned Psychiatrist, Peter Breggin MD, on adverse reactions to medications, discusses in depth the science and end results of adverse reactions to psychiatric medications. This text should be read by anyone taking or prescribing medication. I have personally spoken with psychiatrists, who work with military personnel, who have informed me they changed the way they currently treat their patients (reducing their use of medication) after hearing Dr. Breggin speak about adverse effects of psychiatric medication.

At the 17th Annual International Military and Civilian Combat Stress conference in May 2009, everyone attending the conference heard an Army social worker state that the use of psychiatric medication on the battlefield was rampant. She had completed two one-year tours of duty in Iraq and Afghanistan and estimated that 90 percent of the U.S. combatants have used, at one time or other, psychiatric medications. She explained that they are being handed out, not only by physicians but also by physicians assistants, nurses, medics and even from soldier to soldier. She was told by various psychiatrists, while deployed, to support medicating troops and in one instance that her services on the battlefield were useless since she could not prescribe medication.

At the same combat stress conference, an U.S. lieutenant colonel commander described how some of his troops, after returning to Germany from Iraq, were given psychiatric medications and how their behavior deteriorated after receiving the medications. Prescriptions for all TRICARE beneficiaries, according to a DoD claims database, indicate that in 2002 a total of 3,739,914 prescriptions for antidepressants and antipsychotics were issued. In 2008 the number of these prescriptions rose to 6,413,035.

In 2009, the number of suicides in the military surpassed the civilian death rate from suicide. The suicide death rate for military personnel was 20.2 per 100,000 while the civilian death rate was 19.2 per 100,000. Veterans between the ages of 20 to 24 had a suicide death rate of 22.9 per100, 000, which is 4 times higher than non-vets the same age. It should also be noted that statistics indicate that there are 10 failed attempts at suicide for each actual completed suicide. This is the first time in decades that military suicides are at the current level. Presently we now have the highest level of suicides in the military that we have seen in three decades. Since 2001 there have been 2,100 suicides in the military, triple the number of troops that have died in Afghanistan and half of all U.S. deaths in Iraq. The correlation of increased suicides, as well as homicides, in the military, and the increased use of medications, with a side effect of suicide, irritability, hostility and aggressiveness does not appear to be a coincidence, but a direct link to adverse reactions a person may experience when taking these medications.

Overall conclusions of the study indicated that approximately 46 percent of people taking these medications committed suicide. The study found a direct link between the use of psychiatric medication as described above and suicide. There are many other studies that cite similar and even more significant findings, but since I don't consider myself an expert in the science of these medications, I will defer all questions in regard to the science behind these medications to Peter Breggin, MD, who will provide extensive testimony in this area. Dr. Breggin has a prestigious background with the National Institute of Mental

Health (NIMH) and elsewhere, where he researched the science of the medications we are discussing.

Also information on the Internet website www.ssristories.com lists hundreds of civilian and military cases of death, suicide, attempted suicide, that are linked to psychiatric medication. It identifies such cases of sudden death in soldiers taking a combination of psychiatric medications, the May 11, 2009 Iraq mental health clinic shooting where five soldiers were killed by a soldier on psychiatric medication.

On the other side of the coin, I have not observed significant long-term studies that have ever shown any psychiatric medication to be effective in treating post-traumatic stress (PTSD), for which significant prescriptions in the military are written. I am not saying that the FDA hasn't seen research presented to them by pharmaceutical companies, that allowed them to approve these medications for treating PTSD, but am concerned that these studies were less than one would desire to approve treating all our military as well as their families. When positive results are reported, they are typically short-term, not long-term effects.

As a retired military officer and founder and director, of the longest running combat stress conference in the world, I have had the opportunity to talk with numerous active and reserve military personnel and their families. I have also heard presentations from experts from throughout the world on combat stress reactions to combat. As a clinical psychologist and mental health professional for over forty-two years, I have had the opportunity to see patients while in the military (I spent over thirty-three in

USA), as well as in my civilian practice. These experiences have also allowed me to teach classes on combat stress reactions in the military as well as in the civilian community.

I have been honored with military awards and my work has been lauded by DoD officials for developing the International Military and Civilian Combat Stress Conference, as well as other programs.

As a military and as a civilian psychologist, I have had an opportunity to develop first- hand opinions regarding, not only the relationship between psychiatric medications and suicide, but other adverse reactions our military personnel experiences that interfere with their performance on the battlefield and when returning home to their families.

My overall observations and clinical experience leads me to state, emphatically, that integrative treatment approaches in treating combat stress and related problems is more effective in the long run, than prescribing drugs, both as a force multiplier and a money saver.

Integrative approaches such as individual counseling, bio-feedback, guided imagery, progressive relaxation, peer counseling, cognitive-behavioral therapy, virtual reality therapy, implosive therapy, hypnosis, etc. have little or no adverse reactions and there is research that shows them to be effective both short-term and long-term. It should be noted that during the first Persian Gulf War, combat stress chambers were successfully used to reduce stress. This is more that can be said currently of psychiatric medication. A recent book written in 2007 by a world renowned psychologist, Stanley Krippner, PhD and his associate, Daryl S. Paulson, PhD titled *Haunted by Combat*, as well as an Epilogue to this text presently being published in the 2010 paperback, gives extensive examples and findings as to the success of providing integrative mental health treatment protocols.

If one considers that the average cost of a prescription for an antidepressant or antipsychotic can cost anywhere from $25 to $50 each month, then the cost the DoD is billed for so-called mental health prescriptions should likely exceed $2 billion a year. This level of funding could pay for all the mental health professionals needed to provide the integrative treatment programs our military personnel and their families need, with no fear of adverse reactions and every expectation of success. If implemented, there are strong indications that the suicide rate would drop dramatically, as well as the increasing number of soldiers being diagnosed with PTSD and other reactions to combat stress.

During the first Persian Gulf War, I was in a medical unit, the 6252nd U.S. Army Reserve Hospital, which deployed most of its military personal. Upon returning after the war ended, I observed many varied problems among the soldiers. These problems consisted of emotional difficulties, marital difficulties, financial problems, general health problems, legal problems, family problems, and spiritual problems.

What was striking at the time was that most of these problems could have been minimized or completely avoided if the soldiers were better prepared prior to deployment. With the assistance of the commanding general of the 6252nd and the staff of our combat stress company, I developed a readiness protocol to address all of the issues one had to deal with prior to and when actually deployed, as well as when returning home. We came up with a 20-minute interviewing manual that, with minimal training, one could administer to each member of a military unit.

The soldier would respond for themselves as well as for their family. The program was called the Human Assistance Rapid Response Team (HARRT brochure attached # 9. and 10.). Members of the combat stress company administered the instrument to military units with significant success. Readiness problems improved and returning prematurely from deployment dropped. The HARRT program also identified suicide ideation and homicide ideation.

Out of the HARRT program, a 2-day conference was born to teach how the HARRT program could be utilized and improved. This conference led to an annual National Tri-Service Combat Stress Conference held for 15 years at Camp Pendleton Marine Base in California. Today this conference, which is held the first week of May, is going into its eighteenth year and has been re-named The Annual International Military and Civilian Combat Stress Conference.

In December of 1997, I was invited to the Pentagon by Brigadier General Richard Lynch to address the Army Reserve Forces Policy Committee's Mobilization Sub-committee in regard to the HARRT program. The committee was made up of seven major generals with command experience. After my presentation of the HARRT program, Major General Donald F. Campbell, Chairman of the Committee stated that the total committee supported the implementation of the HARRT program. Major General Campbell in his letter stated, "As chairman of that mobilization subcommittee, I am pleased that our decision to support your program has assisted you in your commitment to pursue your goal of fully implementing the HARRT Program with all our military services, both Active and Reserve."

A Major General, who was one of the committee members of the above mentioned panel and a Commanding General for the National Guard requested at the committee meeting that the HARRT program be first fully implemented for all members of the National Guard in his state. Since there was no follow-up funding from the DoD to fully implement the HARRT program, this request could not be followed up on at the time. This lack of funding and follow up from DoD was repeated on other occasions resulting in the underutilization of an admittedly viable program. In another instance, a National Guard Special Forces unit in California specifically contacted me to perform the HARRT interviews on all their members prior to deployment. Since there was no funding and orders to honor their request received from DoD, the request could not be implemented. The Special Forces commander was upset and disappointed his request could not be honored and had to deploy knowing his unit could have been better prepared to depart.

On May 28, 1999, I was invited to visit the Department of the Army's Office of the Surgeon General. As a result of the visit, a letter was written (attachment #2) commentating favorably on the combat stress conference, the Prisoner of War Conference and the HARRT program. A comment in the letter specific to the HARRT program is a follows: "It is reasonable to expect that this program alone will directly benefit hundreds of thousands of service members and their families." This comment was related to a then recent DoD directive 6490.5, instructing all military organizations to implement combat stress programs.

From 1997 and later in 1999, when the HARRT program and combat stress conferences were initially supported by the above-mentioned DoD organizations at the Pentagon, there has been little follow-up by DoD to fully follow through and implement these viable combat stress educational and preventative programs. This lack of follow-up has predictably resulted in many hardships for military personnel as well as their families. No one knows how many suicides and homicides could have been averted if these combat stress programs could have been fully implemented back in 1997 or 1999. Instead the DoD has supported the extensive use of psychiatric medication, which appears to have worsened the problems of combat stress, which can be readily measure by the increases in suicide and homicide in the military.

In 2005, the military command, from the Tri-Service Combat Stress Conference founding organization (6252nd USAH), stated it did not have the staff or funding to continue the Tri-Service Combat Stress Conference and asked myself and other retired officers if we could continue the conference privately, with no military funding or support. This request was shocking, due the fact that the need for combat stress training was elevated since the beginning of the War on Terrorism. This lack of support for combat stress training was consistent with the lack of DoD follow-up mentioned above. This challenge to continue the training conference was taken up by a few dedicated retired officers and today the conference still continues and is now the longest running and in my mind, one of the best conferences held in the world on combat stress. It should be noted that in 1999, when I visited the DoD to discuss the conference, I suggested that the DoD take over the conference due to the important nature of the content and the fact that when I retired I was fearful the conference would not continue. I was told that I was doing a good job both verbally and in writing but that they were not interested in assuming leadership of the conference.

To date, the International Civilian and Military Combat Stress Conference have trained thousands of military and civilian personnel on how to effectively deal with combat stress related problems. It has also motivated other military and civilian groups to start their own conferences on combat stress. It is considered by many to be the gold standard of all combat stress conferences, as demonstrated by the many world-renowned military and civilian instructors and federal and state legislative people who have attended and have given presentations over the years.[78]

At the onset of the current War on Terrorism, many expert presenters at the combat stress conference warned that military personnel should not be medicated when on the battlefields

---

78   Tri-Service Combat Stress Conference. (n.d.). Retrieved November 1, 2015, from http://www.tservcsc.bizhosting.com

or when eventually returning home. The overall consensus of presenters, as well as people attending the conference, was that integrative treatment was the most effective way of dealing with combat stress issues. I would estimate that only 2 percent of people attending the conference advocated medicating soldiers. This 2 percent consisted primarily of psychiatrists. It should be noted that most psychiatrists are primarily trained to administer medication and generally don't have the training to provide integrative treatment. This lack of exposure to integrative treatment can be traced back to the medical schools that train psychiatrists.

I have personally seen military personnel as patients, who explained that they were given antidepressants on the battlefield to simply try to stop smoking. One Marine explained to me that when he returned back home, he could find no indication in his medical record that he was ever given psychiatric medication. He experienced cognitive problems from the first time he was given the medication and when he complained to the medical staff, he was given even more psychiatric medication. It wasn't until he, on his own, took himself off the medication after two years that he returned to normal functioning. This Marine was interviewed by me and California Assemblyperson Mary Salas' (Chair of Assembly Veterans Committee) chief of staff, Francisco Estrada, to evaluate veteran's services in California. This is not an isolated case since I have encountered many military personnel with the same experiences. The use of the psychiatric medications is prevalent on the battlefield, where it is being dispensed not only by medical doctors but also by physician's assistants, medics, soldier to soldier.

Since the War on Terrorism began, there has been a steady increase in suicide and homicide in the military. There has also been a steady increase in the number of psychiatric medications purchased by DoD and prescribed to military personnel and their families. Research and the FDA (black box warning) have revealed that there is a direct relationship between the use of psychiatric medication and suicide. The black box warnings on the actual medication label also describe the link between the medication and suicide, as well as other cognitive effects, which can also trigger homicidal behavior.

There have been integrative treatment training programs, as well as actual treatment protocols, available since the end of the first Persian Gulf War that have been effective in treating and identifying residual effects of combat stress i.e. the Human Assistance Rapid Response Team (HARRT), Tri-Service Combat Stress Conference. These programs have been underutilized and underfunded in favor of wide spread use of psychiatric medications with the result being increases in military suicide and homicide. A solution to the ongoing and increasing problems with suicide and homicide is not more medication but more integrative treatment programs administered by trained mental health providers, as well as military leadership personnel.

The full implementation of the HARRT program as a readiness tool, as well as its use as an instrument to identify potential suicide and homicide ideation is advisable. The HARRT program was recognized by DoD personnel as a valuable tool, as far back as 1997 and 1999, with recommendations at that time to fully implement the program.

Also DoD should recognize that all military personnel in combat experience post-traumatic stress (PTS)–notice there is not a "D" at the end. PTS for military personnel is a normal reaction to being in an abnormal environment, the battlefield. PTS becomes a disorder (D) when the soldier (term referring to individuals in all military organizations), does not learn ways of dealing with the PTS and how to normalizing themselves. If this normalization process does not occur, then the soldier can develop a disorder and the PTS can become post-traumatic stress disorder (PTSD).

It is critical that the DoD become aware of the difference between PTS and PTSD. If DoD can recognize that psychiatric medication has not been effective in treating combat stress, than a natural conclusion would be to turn their focus and finances to methods that have been approved and worked in the past to various degrees and expanding these programs. One program that should be strongly considered for implementation by DoD should be a mandatory one (1) hour a day program for thirty (30) days for all military personnel returning from combat zones. This mandatory one hour a day, of structured mental training (MT), administered by trained staff, using a military wide standardized approach, will help all returning soldiers realize that they are having normal reactions from being in an abnormal battlefield environment. By learning methods of dealing with abnormal experiences and developing coping approaches through integrative treatment methods, they can return to normal functioning. There will no longer be a need for soldiers to hide what they are experiencing since all individuals, by attending mandatory MT programs, will realize that they are all human beings, in a similar situation, subjected to the same stresses and similar experiences.

Cutting back on the extensive use of psychiatric medication and implementing integrative programs such as the HARRT program, MT programs and similar programs throughout the military, could lead to strong expectations for significant decreases in PTSD, suicide and homicide in the military. This decrease would result in more soldiers being available for deployment, reduction in family and personal hardships and a reduction in psychiatric disability monies being spent, while in the military as well as when the soldier returns to civilian life after discharge.

(End of Congressional Testimony I Submitted)

As one would expect, the American Psychological Association, the American Psychiatric Association, and Big Pharma also attended the above-mentioned hearings. They defended their position for the use of psychiatric medications. One of my major disappointments as a certified psychologist is that the American Psychological Association has bought into the idea of utilizing psychiatric medication in conjunction with psychotherapy. It has always been my contention that it is much more difficult to be successful with psychotherapy if an individual is taking a brain-altering medication; it's similar to trying to work with someone who is intoxicated and expecting them to benefit from talk therapy while they are drunk in the therapist's office. I personally feel that integrative treatment offers psychologists many more tools to help patients with emotional disorders than traditional psychiatry, which often relies on medications.

From the time of the congressional hearings up until 2015, some progress has been made in the form of numerous professional and newspaper articles, discussing the subject of suicide in the military and civilian community and its correlation to the adverse effects of psychiatric medication.

CHAPTER 6

RECOMMENDATIONS FOR EFFECTIVE MENTAL HEALTH TREATMENT: INTEGRATIVE WELLNESS PROGRAMS FOR VETERANS AND CIVILIANS

The integrative medicine/wellness treatment modality was poignantly observed in 2012 at the International Military and Civilian Combat Stress Conference held in Pasadena, California. We had a lieutenant colonel (LTC) from the Army arrive in a wheelchair an hour early for the conference. He immediately sought me out and expressed a strong need to talk with me about his situation prior to the start of the conference. He had shrapnel wounds to his legs and feet, which had resulted in a large ulcer on one foot. He mentioned that when he went to the Veterans Administration Hospital, he was told that his foot had to be amputated. He also indicated he was diagnosed with post-traumatic stress disorder (PTSD), which caused nightmares, depression, and other symptoms associated with PTSD, and was given a combination of psychiatric medications for this condition. He appeared very depressed and indicated he had thoughts of suicide. He was having family problems, and while he had previously owned several houses, due to his physical and mental condition he had lost those properties. He asked if I had any recommendations to help improve his situation.

As a result of attending all five days of lectures and meeting privately with most of the presenters, the LTC walked out of the conference without the use of his wheelchair. One of the presenters exposed him to non-medical treatment options for pain, which appeared to provide some relief to the LTC. He had a much smaller bandage on his foot and felt much more positive than when he had first arrived. He was given the names of specialists to follow up with and was told that there was treatment available for his foot that would preclude amputation. He was also given the phone numbers of the people he spoke with at the conference.

At so many of the combat stress conferences, I always feel that if I had all of the expert conference presenters in their fields of expertise present in one clinic, it would be the best clinic in the world for working with our veterans. My observation of the above-mentioned LTC supports this continuing premise that integrative treatment works much better than any psychiatric medication. This continued experience of success in working with severely injured people is not new for me, since I observed these kinds of successes when working in the Department of Physical Medicine and Rehabilitation at the UC Davis Medical Center. It's amazing how successful a comprehensive PM&R program, also at times known more or less now as integrative medicine or integrative wellness, can be.

The physician that usually oversees PM&R is called a physiatrist. Many people, including medical doctors, are not familiar with the term physiatrist, which translates to "physical physician" in Greek. This type of treatment approach goes back many centuries and has been practiced in many cultures. In the 1970s I had the opportunity to work in PM&R as chief of professional services and assistant director at the UC Davis Medical Center, which allowed me to work with patients suffering from physical and emotional impairments such as spinal cord injuries, muscle diseases, burn injuries, brain damage, gunshot injuries, strokes, and diabetes. One can see from the impairments how this specialty, in the United States, grew out of prior wars.

Treatment providers in PM&R also have a wide range of specialties, including physiatry, physical therapy (PT), occupational therapy (OT), speech therapy (ST), orthotics / prosthetics, psychosocial and vocational (PSV) specialties (which are different from general mental health providers), rehabilitation nursing, and biomedical engineers. The PM&R specialists developed many varied treatment modalities to effectively work with their patients. It was not unusual to see patients receiving treatments beyond the standard PT, OT, and ST. Routinely applied were modalities such as hypnosis, biofeedback, acupuncture, guided imagery, relaxation exercises, hydrotherapy, brain retraining exercises, psychosocial vocational testing, nutrition counseling, spiritual counseling, family support, and general psychological counseling.

Today, we see many people, including those with impairments and those who want to sustain a mentally healthy lifestyle, in need of the various PM&R treatment modalities. Treatment programs that go beyond traditional PM&R and are not exclusively for physically impaired individuals are now being called integrative wellness programs.

Here is a protocol for a person entering a wellness program that I developed and is supported by a close associate, Chrisanne Gordon, MD – physiatrist:

- A complete physical examination by a physician (preferably a physiatrist).

- A complete psychological, social, and vocational evaluation.

- A program coordinator (PC) will be assigned for each person.

- A complete individually tailored wellness (ITW) program will be given to the person by their PC describing the various wellness modalities they will be scheduled to participate in. Modalities include exercise, biofeedback, yoga, relaxation exercises, guided imagery, breath program, nutrition, supplements, vocational planning, and spiritual counseling.

- A meeting will occur on a regular weekly basis with the patient, PC, occasionally therapy specialists to discuss progress being made by the patient.

- If it is determined by the physician and staff that various medications a person may be taking are resulting in adverse reactions and interfering with their wellness, then recommendations for medication changes will occur; in the case of psychiatric medications or non-prescribed drugs, a detox program will be planned.[79]

This overall concept has been proven, in part, over the years, but this concept looks at a one-stop wellness program that covers all aspects of wellness in one facility.

INTEGRATIVE TREATMENT/ WELLNESS MODALITIES

Throughout the course of my career, I find the treatment of choice for PTS, or at times PTSD, is integrative treatment/wellness. Choices of treatment can be incorporated with each other and include the following:

---

79 Gordon, C. (2013, December 4). Why Medicine Alone Can't Help Our Veterans. Retrieved November 19, 2015, from http://www.huffingtonpost.com/chrisanne-gordon/why-medicine-alone-cant-help-our-veterans_b_4386587.html

Cognitive Behavioral Therapy (CBT): This can be a short-term psychotherapy program, and it is commonly used to treat emotional disorders. It focuses on solving present problems and making better choices by changing thought and behavior patterns. CBT helps a person stay in the present and focus on resolving current problems. It focuses on making a plan to do better that requires action from the client with guidance from the therapist. I have found Reality Therapy to be the treatment of choice for residual effects of combat stress.[80]

Hypnosis: I have successfully used hypnosis with my patients while working at a university teaching hospital in the division of physical medicine and rehabilitation. By having an individual heighten his or her focus and concentration, one can see positive results—not only in the patient's ability to reduce stress but also in his or her ability to relax muscles. This allows the physical therapist to be more effective in treating the patient. In this therapy, the patient concentrates intensely on a specific thought or memory, which therapist guides the patient through, thereby enabling the patient to block out sources of distraction. Hypnotized subjects can increase their response to suggestions, which can help them to relax when thinking about a traumatic event from the past. Teaching an individual autohypnosis is constructive because the person can perfect this process long after therapy concludes.[81]

---

80   In-Depth: Cognitive Behavioral Therapy. (n.d.). Retrieved November 14, 2015, from http://psychcentral.com/lib/in-depth-cognitive-behavioral-therapy/
81   Definition of Hypnosis. (n.d.). Retrieved November 14, 2015, from http://www.asch.net/public/generalinfoonhypnosis/definitionofhypnosis.aspx

Relaxation Therapy: This is a procedure or activity that helps a person decrease mental and physical tension. I have found Jacobson Progressive Relaxation techniques to be effective with veterans I have worked with over the years. The technique involves learning to monitor tension in each specific muscle group in the body by deliberately inducing tension in each group. The tension is then released, with attention paid to the contrast between tension and relaxation. When I was the commanding officer of a reserve unit that was going to deployed, I took the 300 stressed people in the unit out for a walk, had them lay on a grassy knoll, and taught them this relaxation technique. Upon returning from deployment, many said they used it effectively to reduce stress.[82]

Deep Breathing: Deep breathing (also known as diaphragmatic breathing, abdominal breathing, belly breathing, and paced respiration) aids in reducing physical and emotional tension. Deep abdominal breathing encourages full oxygen exchange for outgoing carbon dioxide, and it has the potential to reduce heartrate and lower or stabilize blood pressure. I prefer the 4-7-8 technique, where you inhale for 4 seconds, hold the breath for 7 seconds, and exhale for 8 seconds.[83]

Meditation: There are many varieties of meditation, yet all of these techniques are designed to promote relaxation and build

---

82   Jacobson, E. (1929). *Progressive relaxation; a physiological and clinical investigation of muscular states and their significance in psychology and medical practice.* Chicago, Ill.: The University of Chicago Press.
83   Kim, S., Schneider, S., Bevans, M., Kravitz, L., Mermier, C., Qualls, C., & Burge, M. (n.d.). PTSD Symptom Reduction With Mindfulness-Based Stretching and Deep Breathing Exercise: Randomized Controlled Clinical Trial of Efficacy. *Journal of Clinical Endocrinology & Metabolism,* 2984-2992.

better energy. The focus of meditation is to effortlessly sustain a singularly-focused form of concentration. The word "meditation" comes from the Latin word "meditari," which means to concentrate.

For years I observed my mother-in-law, Julia Krutlies, pray and say the rosary. She would do this on a daily basis. She always appeared free of stress and lived to be one hundred and two and a half. I believe that her ability to meditate in prayer was one contributing factor in her long and fruitful life. She was truly a gift and inspiration to the world; through her example, she made the value of meditative prayer clear to everyone around her.

Tai Chi and Qigong: In the book *Tai Chi and Qi Gong*, these ancient arts are described as "two mind-body practices that originated in ancient China. Practiced widely in China for thousands of years, both have become popular in the West. People of almost any age or condition can participate in them. Many people who practice tai chi and Qigong report heightened feelings of well-being along with a variety of other health benefits. Practiced in a variety of styles, tai chi involves slow, gentle movements, deep breathing, and meditation. The meditation is sometimes called 'moving meditation.' This type of low-impact, weight-bearing, and aerobic and relaxing exercise began as a martial art. As it developed, it took on the purpose of enhancing physical and mental health."[84]

Qigong: According to the National Qigong Association, Qigong (pronounced chee gong) focuses on regulated breathing,

---

84   Kron, J. (2005). Tai Chi and Qi Gong.

exercises consisting of slow, circular movements, focused meditation, and self-massage.[85] Qigong is believed to relax the mind,
muscles, tendons, joints, and inner organs -- helping to improve
circulation, relieve stress and pain, and restore health. It's practiced widely in China's clinics and hospitals. Some believe that as
a complement to Western medicine, Qigong can help the body
heal itself, slowing or even reversing the effects of certain conditions. For example, one research study revealed that after just
ten weeks of Qigong practice, participants enjoyed significantly
lower blood pressure levels (both diastolic and systolic).[86]

Guided Imagery: This ancient technique has been practiced for centuries, and indigenous groups like the Navajo Indi-
ans enjoyed the benefits of this simple practice. Guided imagery
is a form of hypnosis in which patients use various forms of
mental imagery to help them deal with both physical and mental
stressors in life. It is also effective with helping veterans with
nightmares.[87]

Prolonged Exposure therapy (PE): This behavior modi-
fication technique has a component called systematic desensitization. It was designed to treat various emotionally upsetting
experiences and, for many years, PTSD symptoms. The focus is
to have the person re-experience the traumatic event by remem-
bering it through guided imagery. It can also take the form of

---

85   http://nqa.org/about-nqa/what-is-qigong/
86   Effects of Qigong on blood pressure, blood pressure determinants and ventilatory func-
      tion in middle-aged patients with essential hypertension. (n.d.). Retrieved November 19,
      2015, from http://www.ncbi.nlm.nih.gov/pubmed/12943180
87   Jain, S., Mcmahon, G., Hasen, P., Kozub, M., Porter, V., King, R., & Guarneri, E. (n.d.).
      Healing Touch With Guided Imagery for PTSD in Returning Active Duty Military: A
      Randomized Controlled Trial. *Military Medicine,* 1015-1021.

physically revisiting the situation that created the stress. This technique can also be referred to as flooding.[88]

However, when utilizing prolonged exposure therapy, one must be cautious; the soldier may not want to talk about his or her experiences or relive them. If the person isn't ready to talk, it can potentially be better for that person to hold off on PE. The general findings of a study printed in the Journal of Nervous and Mental Diseases revealed that U.S. Army veterans who repressed trauma, as opposed to talking about it, experienced no additional health problems and had a life expectancy equal to other veterans. Also, the study indicated that veterans who repressed memories of trauma were less likely to exhibit symptoms of post–traumatic stress disorder.[89] Charles Figley, PhD, founder of the Traumatology Institute (Tulane University) and one of the co-authors of the above-mentioned study stated, "It's the ability to compartmentalize information in a way that you can handle … [and] if people discuss traumas before they feel ready, it could lead to even deeper suffering."[90] Figley encourages therapists to only explore prolonged exposure therapy when the patient is ready and willing to discuss the trauma.[91]

---

88   Foa, E., & Hembree, E. (2007). *Prolonged exposure therapy for PTSD: Emotional processing of traumatic experiences: Therapist guide.* Oxford: Oxford University Press.
89   Repression Can be GOOD! - charlesfigley. (n.d.). Retrieved November 8, 2015, from https://sites.google.com/site/charlesfigley/Home/repression-can-be-good

90   Repression Can be GOOD! - charlesfigley. (n.d.). Retrieved November 8, 2015, from https://sites.google.com/site/charlesfigley/Home/repression-can-be-good

91   Repression Can be GOOD! - charlesfigley. (n.d.). Retrieved November 8, 2015, from https://sites.google.com/site/charlesfigley/Home/repression-can-be-good

Eye Movement Desensitization and Reprocessing (EMDR): EMDR therapy "facilitates the accessing and processing of traumatic memories and other adverse life experience to bring these to an adaptive resolution. After successful treatment … affective distress is relieved, negative beliefs are reformulated, and physiological arousal is reduced. [During EMDR], the client attends to emotionally disturbing material in brief sequential doses while simultaneously focusing on an external stimulus [along with directed eye movements]."[92]

Peer Support Groups: There are many veteran peer support groups that focus on helping each other cope with life problems. This is done by sharing experiences and talking about what coping techniques seem to be helpful. In WWII, the long ship ride home could take a week or more; during this time, many informal peer groups developed where soldiers shared experiences and told each other how they dealt with issues. In therapy, it is critical that a formal peer group have an experienced leader or two to be most effective.

Biofeedback: This is a technique that I discovered in the mid 1970s that I found effective with my PM&R patients at the medical school's teaching hospital where I worked. Biofeedback uses guided imagery along with actual measured physical responses revealed by the biofeedback equipment. This therapy allows the person to become aware of, and eventually control,

92   What is EMDR? | EMDR Institute – Eye Movement Desensitization and Reprocessing Therapy. (n.d.). Retrieved November 8, 2015, from http://www.emdr.com/what-is-emdr/

some of his or her physical functions and responses.[93] Some of the processes that can be controlled include brainwave activity, body temperature in extremities, muscle tension, and pain perception.[94]

Acupuncture: I personally observed the efficacy of acupuncture in the 1970s when working at the teaching hospital I previously mentioned. Although it has been used for decades with patients, it wasn't until 1997 that it was formally recognized as a legitimate medical technique at the Conference of the National Institute of Health Consensus Development. There are many conditions that can be treated by acupuncture; one of the conditions we used it for at the PM&R department I worked in was pain. Other uses would include treatment for the residual effects of combat stress and for addiction to legally prescribed psychiatric medications or illegal drugs. Acupuncture is incredibly beneficial because it can reduce the physical and emotional withdrawal when combined with other integrative approaches.

Equine Therapy: In this therapy, therapists support patients as they interact with horses. This experiential method has recently proven to be very effective in working with veterans based on the presentations made at the International Military and Civilian Combat Stress Conference. Horses exhibit behaviors similar to humans, and these commonalities allow the veteran to connect with the horse. It is believed that horses can sense the emotional

---

93   Relaxation Techniques for Health: What You Need To Know. (n.d.). Retrieved November 8, 2015, from https://nccih.nih.gov/health/stress/relaxation.htm

94   Biofeedback. (n.d.). Retrieved November 8, 2015, from http://medical-dictionary.thefree-dictionary.com/Biofeedback (psychology)

state of the person they are involved with. Therefore, the feedback the horse provides can be insightful to the person (almost like a biofeedback machine).[95]

Exercise: Thomas Jefferson stated, "Walking is the best possible exercise. Habituate yourself to walk very far."[96] Aerobic exercise not only improves the cardiovascular system, but also helps the brain develop more neuropathways. *Positive Addiction* by William Glasser, MD, explains this in detail. In addition, people often state that they think more clearly when exercising. Group exercising also enhances social involvement in a very cooperative manner (i.e. team sports). I remember a veteran stating that when he was playing basketball, it felt good and made him feel like he was getting back to normal.

Nutrition: Proper diet results in good physical and mental health. Well over 50 percent of American men and women are overweight. This results in many physical and accompanying emotional difficulties. An appropriate, balanced diet is critical for veterans returning from combat so they can move on with their life without additional distractions that will prevent them from returning to where they want to be. Most veterans experience a state of high physical well-being in the military that they are proud of; if they return home and gain weight and lose stamina from a poor diet, this can be very discouraging in their civilian life.

---

95   EAGALA Primary site. (n.d.). Retrieved November 14, 2015, from http://www.eagala.org/Information/What_Is_EAP_EAL

96   https://www.monticello.org/site/research-and-collections/exercise

Yoga: The physical postures of yoga are useful in reducing an individual's stress level and developing core spinal strength and flexibility. Yoga is seen by many as a complete exercise program and physical therapy extension.[97]

Pilates: Pilates is a controlled movements program, which becomes a physical workout when properly performed. If practiced with consistency, Pilates has the potential to improve flexibility, build core strength, and develop control and endurance. It emphasizes alignment, breathing, core strength, and improving coordination and balance.[98]

Hyperbaric Oxygen Therapy (HBOT): HBOT has been utilized in Physical Medicine And Rehabilitation for decades, to repair injured cellular damage from ulcers and wounds. HBOT works by bringing oxygen to the damaged cellular areas, which then promotes healing. A healthy brain uses 100% of the oxygen the body provides it. However, when there is trauma causing cellular damage to the brain, it needs extra oxygen to heal. HBOT provides that extra oxygen which expedites healing.[99]

Reconsolidation of Traumatic Memories (RTM): "The RTM protocol is a non-drug, cognitive therapy that reprograms the neurological connection between the brains feeling center

97   A Beginner's Guide to the History of Yoga | Yoga for Beginners. (2007, August 28). Retrieved November 14, 2015, from http://www.yogajournal.com/article/beginners/the-roots-of-yoga/

98   Pilates. (n.d.). Retrieved November 14, 2015, from http://www.pilates.com/BBAPP/V/pilates/origins-of-pilates.html

99   Hyperbaric oxygen therapy. (n.d.). Retrieved November 14, 2015, from http://www.mayoclinic.org/tests-procedures/hyperbaric-oxygen-therapy/basics/definition/prc-20019167

and specific traumatic memories. It is best described as a relaxed re-imaging procedure."[100]

Critical Incident Stress Management (CISM): In a letter to me, Jeff Mitchell, PhD, founder of CISM, he described CISM as

> an approach to managing traumatic exposures. It has a forty-year positive track record of assisting military personnel, police, fire, rescue and emergency medical personnel and others who have experienced traumatic events. It is not psychotherapy or a substitute for psychotherapy. It is a psycho-educational program designed to prepare people for a trauma exposure and to assist them in a rapid return to normal life functions in the aftermath of traumatic experience. It has its greatest positive effects when used as an integral part of a continuum-of-care that ranges from pre-trauma preparations to referrals for appropriate psychotherapy when necessary.
>
> CISM is built on and is consistent with the foundational concept resistance, resilience and recovery. Resistance refers to psychological immunity. CISM helps to build resistance by means of pre-incident education, as well as the encouragement of healthy living and enhanced lifestyle behaviors and attitudes before a traumatic

---

100   PTSD. (n.d.). Retrieved November 8, 2015, from http://www.courageheartwisdom.com/PTSD.html

event strikes. CISM, in addition, promotes stress management education and the practice of stress management skills. CISM encourages the buildup of protective factors such as self-esteem, optimism, improved nutrition, appropriate sleep habits, social support, exercise, family life, and avoidance of harmful substances.

Despite the fact that there is a growing number of positive outcome CISM studies, including randomized control trials both within the military and in civilian areas, military psychiatric leadership has resisted and sometimes openly opposed the utilization of CISM programs within the military in favor medicating veterans. Such a narrow view of effective interventions places veterans at greater risk of becoming stuck in a traumatized state.[101]

Physical Medicine & Rehabilitation Program (PM&R): I have discussed PM&R in other chapters, but I am repeating it here because it is such a valuable asset to our veterans. Involvement in PM&R can be on an inpatient or outpatient basis, depending on the need. When there is a physical injury involved, I see PM&R as the initial treatment of choice. It consists of various specialties such as physical therapy, occupational therapy, speech therapy, orthotics/prosthetics, psychological, social, and vocational services, biomedical engineering, and rehabilitation nursing. Within these specialty areas, the various types of other treatment

---

101   http://www.info-trauma.org/flash/media-e/mtichellCriticalIncidentStressManagement.pdf

modalities can be incorporated into the PM&R program. Ideally, the director of the PM&R program should be a physician with a specialty in physiatry.[102]

Digital Storytelling: I find that this relatively new technique appears to be a modern derivative of psychodrama (developed by Jacob Marino, MD). When I was in undergraduate school, we took a field trip to New York City to observe Dr. Marino demonstrating psychodrama in his storefront office. I witnessed it as group psychotherapy, where people were doing role playing with each other and acting as important characters in their lives. As explained to me by founder Ben Patton, "It is an action method, often used as a psychotherapy, in which clients use spontaneous dramatization, role-playing, and dramatic self-presentation to investigate and gain insight on how to improve their lives. Similar to psychodrama, Digital Story Telling includes elements of theater, often conducted on a production set, where props can be used. By closely recreating past, present and future real-life situations and acting them out in front of video cameras, individuals have the opportunity to evaluate their behavior and more deeply understand a particular situation in their lives."

Ben Patton explains the following: "Patton Veterans Project, Inc. now provides therapeutic filmmaking to help veterans and military families cope with post-traumatic stress. Their signature 'I WAS THERE' (IWT) film workshops enable veterans to connect with one another and their families, make sense of traumatic expe-

---

102   Association of Academic Physiatrists. (n.d.). Retrieved November 14, 2015, from http://www.physiatry.org/

riences, and substantially reduce their symptoms of PTS. IWT workshops combine the therapeutic value of storytelling with digital video, the communications medium of choice for today's generation of veterans. The filmmaking program encourages collaboration, reduces stigma, and builds hope and a renewed sense of community. Veteran participants have called the workshop an 'ice-breaker' that enabled them to reclaim their personal narrative and move forward in healing and transition to civilian life."

Patton Veterans Project was founded in 2012 by Benjamin Patton, grandson of WWII's General George S. Patton, Jr. and son of Major General George S. Patton IV. Ben has applied a graduate degree in developmental psychology and two decades of experience in filmmaking to serve the military in a unique way.

There are other forms of integrative treatment that you may encounter that are also effective in helping our vets get back to normal lives. The most successful ones involve working with caring people in one way or another. This is the common thread that works in all successful approaches.[103]

The Vital Warrior™ Program: This is a combined treatment of some of the specialties described above. A former Navy SEAL, Mikal A. Vega, described to me how getting off psychiatric medications and turning toward various integrative treatment modalities saved his life. As a result, he developed a program for veterans based on the various treatment modalities that were effective for him.

---

103   I WAS THERE Films - Listen. Collaborate. Empower. (n.d.). Retrieved November 14, 2015, from http://iwastherefilms.org/

Below is a description provided by the Vital Warrior™ program:

> VitalWarrior.org is a non-profit organization and a system of non-pharmaceutical rebalancing designed by retired Navy SEAL Mikal A. Vega, to alleviate the detrimental effects of acute stress in its clients.
>
> The mission of Vital Warrior™ is to develop decompression centers within close proximity to a military base where services will be accessible to all. Each vital warrior center will provide integrative alternative therapies that address trauma on a brain–body basis. The philosophy is to provide clients with nonpharmaceutical solutions to healing, including hands-on therapy, knowledge and skills to regaining a reconnection from within through hormonal rebalancing. Veterans suffering from PTS and TBI often distance themselves from their families, friends and themselves. What they need is a personalized approach to their healing. Vital Warrior™'s vision and mission is to help clients reconnect to their lives, their families and their community.[104]

Another outstanding integrative treatment program, which does not use brain altering psychiatric medications, is called OPERATION: TOHIDU located at Melwood. Their complete history and program description is reprinted with permission below:

---

[104] FAR INFRA RED SPECTRUM THERAPY. (n.d.). Retrieved November 14, 2015, from http://vitalwarrior.org/

Melwood Background

Melwood started in 1963 when a small group of parents and supporters decided to teach plant care to young adults who were considered by most to be untrainable, and unemployable. Their goal was almost unheard of: jobs for people with "disabilities." On seven acres of unimproved land - donated by Andrew's Air Force Base - Melwood's founders pitched an Army surplus tent and began to lay the infrastructure for a place where people with differing abilities could learn good work habits, gain specific job skills and earn self-generated income. Over the following decades, Melwood would pioneer many new milestones in the field that would be known as social-entrepreneurial ventures: businesses with the "double bottom line" of providing revenue as well as jobs and independence for people with differing abilities.

Melwood is a 501(c)(3) nonprofit charitable organization. We are one of the ten largest nonprofit agencies of the nearly 600 U.S. AbilityOne Program affiliated agencies nationwide. We provide jobs and job supports, career training, life skills improvements, community supports and recreational services for over 1,900 people with differing abilities each year, including many veterans and wounded warfighters. Melwood employs more than 1,460 people, including nearly 800 workers with differing abilities. We deliver essential facilities services to over 40 military bases (including 26 military Commands) and federal agencies in the DC metropolitan region, including Fort George G. Meade, the U.S. Naval Academy, Aberdeen Proving Ground, Washington Navy Yard, U.S. Naval Observatory, Marine Corp Base Quantico, Naval Air Station Patuxent River, Naval Research Lab, Joint Base

Anacostia-Bolling, Goddard Space Flight Center, USDA, HUD, and The Kennedy Center for the Performing Arts.[105]

Melwood also offers an amazing program, "Operation: Tohidu" (also reprinted below with permission):

Operation: Tohidu is an experiential reintegration program designed for the growing population of warfighters who are living with post-traumatic stress, mild-to-moderate traumatic brain Injury and other deployment-related traumas. It is a holistic retreat where veterans are able to share a common experience and heal in a safe environment.

In a peaceful and secluded atmosphere, participants connect with nature and their fellow war fighters to become empowered to better manage anxiety and post-traumatic stress. At Melwood's 108-acre Retreat and Recreation Center in Southern, Maryland, guests participate in a combination of educational and experiential activities utilizing a strict program model, reminiscent of military structure. Guests are welcomed from around the county. Any veteran or active duty service member who has been diagnosed or is self-reporting with post-traumatic stress or other deployment related trauma is eligible to attend. No referral is required. The weeklong retreat is free of charge to active and veteran service members, including accommodations and travel.

Education sessions seek to empower participants so they are no longer at the mercy of a "system" or providers who know

---

105   Our History: Melwood. (n.d.). Retrieved November 8, 2015, from https://www.melwood.org/about/our-history
Reprinted with permission.

very little about combat-related PTS (d) – even though they are often being asked to treat it. Participants will learn and better understand the clinical criteria, how it gets diagnosed, what the long term prognosis is, how to make it better, how to make it worse, what interventions work, what kind of support is available. They will be educated specifically to combat-related PTS (d), which is different from the civilian version, and complicated by military training, culture and operational tempo. Operation: Tohidu's goal is to make each participant a "Subject Matter Expert" on his or her own condition.

Short-term outcomes:

- Keep the veteran or service member in the workforce. In the case of active duty personnel, maintain or return them to a fit for full duty status
- Decrease in subjective experience of anxiety and/or depression
- Improved sense of personal mastery of lives and triggering situations
- Change in expectations
- Establishment of support system via relationship with other participants
- Ability to make informed decisions with respect to psychopharmacological and other interventions: remediate fully informed consent
- Prevention of further psychological decline
- Completion of smoking cessation and other substance abuse treatment program
- Modeling of health and wellness lifestyle

INVISIBLE SCARS

Long-term outcomes:

- Unemployed veterans will be able to return to the workforce; increase the likelihood that they will remain employed. Active duty personnel will remain fit for duty or return to full duty if they have been in a limited duty status
- "Symptom" relief, mitigation, and management
- Continued execution of improvement plan developed during the retreat
- Continued education about trauma responses and coping strategies
- Increase in inter-personal relationships as a source of ongoing support
- Ability to maintain a wellness lifestyle
- Ability to integrate and fully function in civilian life[106]

---

106 Operation: Tohidu. (n.d.). Retrieved November 8, 2015, from http://www.operationtohi-du.org/Melwood_tohidu_brochure.pdf
Reprinted with permission.

CHAPTER 7

REALITY THERAPY/ CHOICE THEORY

THE GOOD, THE BAD, AND THE UGLY: THE TRUTH ABOUT MENTAL HEALTH PROVIDERS

Although this chapter's main focus is on Reality Therapy/ Choice Theory Psychology, the secondary focus is on psychiatry's role in mental health treatment programs; in the military and civilian world, psychiatry is in charge of most mental health treatment programs. Psychiatrists generally supervise most other professionals who provide mental health treatment in facilities. Over the past three decades, psychiatry has turned to primarily administering psychiatric medications and I want to show the difference between the now-standard psychiatric practices that revolve around psychiatric medications as a primary treatment and practitioners of Reality Therapy/ Choice Theory Psychology (RT/CT), which was founded in the 1960s by a psychiatrist, William Glasser, MD.

Most professions have good and bad people within them but, based on my direct contacts, observations from other people, and written materials, I assign a third class to most psychiatrists—the ugly. If you ask me how I can be so harsh with this classification, my response would be that I consider someone ugly when they contribute directly or indirectly to hurting other people—often by dealing them brain-altering medication that contributes to their suffering and, in severe instances, death by dead-in-bed syndrome, suicide, or homicide).

On the other hand, a good mental health professional significantly helps people lift themselves out of despair to a more healthy and productive lifestyles.

A bad mental health professional doesn't make a difference in people's lives one way or another.

Over the span of five decades in the mental health field, I have run into all three of the mentioned classifications. Here's a more in-depth view of what I experienced from professionals in each classification:

THE GOOD

Psychiatrists such as the founder of Reality Therapy/Choice Theory (RT/CT) Psychology, Dr. William Glasser, are far and few between. They contribute significantly to providing outstanding mental health services that actually lead people to positive mental health outcomes. They not only get deeply involved with the people they work with, but also have a very strong sense of caring for their patients as well as their families.

The *good* therapist is not only a therapist but is also considered a "conditional friend." This is to say that when a patient is with the therapist, the patient feels that they are friends in that specific time period. We all have people in our life who are conditional friends, such as the maître d' at our favorite restaurant, the postal delivery person, the people we work out with at the gym, our neighbor, and the cashier at our local grocery store. A common thread with our conditional friendships is that they make our lives better, even if it's only in that specific environment. They do not do things that make us feel bad or injure us; otherwise they would not be friends.

LEVELS OF FRIENDSHIP/ INVOLVEMENT

One should be aware that the involvement with all our friendships is at different levels. The levels range from the highest, level 1, (which includes our spouse and close family members with whom we can discuss the most intimate aspects of our life) to the lowest, level 5 (which includes acquaintances to whom we merely say hello and smile when we encounter them). In most instances, friends we encounter at work can be seen as a level 3 or 4. At this level, we discuss world news and events, day-to-day activities of work, and minor family life situations. Our closest friends are usually at level 2, where we can discuss our personal feelings about our community and world, as well as what occurs in each of our families.

One of the major things I tell people to be aware of, at any level of friendship, is to never change the level given to another person while actually with that person. There are situations in life where people will talk with you as if you're level 2 friends, and even though you hold them at a level 3 or 4, they expect you to respond as a higher-level friend. In order to avoid potential mistakes involving friendships, I recommend that any change of friendship levels be considered away from the actual person with whom you are considering becoming more involved.

When seeing a psychiatrist or any other type of mental health professional for therapy, you automatically expect that this conditional relationship will be at a level 1 because of the need to get very personal psychological help when talking with them in their office. By doing this, you are giving them complete trust to help you improve the quality of your life. Therefore, if this person is not helping you but indirectly or directly hurting you, it can be devastating—both in and out of therapy.

We give a high degree of trust to the doctors whom we feel will help us improve our life. That's why so often, when a person receives poor treatment from their doctors, it has a devastating effect on their life. This devastation doesn't only happen within a person-to-person relationship, but also happens on an institutional level. In the past, the military's high-ranking leaders have given the profession of psychiatry complete authority for mental health services without question, even as suicide rates remained unacceptably high.

If one continuously fails in the military as a combat officer, they would be removed from their leadership position. The same principle holds true for a civilian executive or CEO whose decisions are costing their company financially. However, this has not happened with the field of psychiatry in the military or in the civilian community (i.e. the VA). When questioned about the significant number of suicides, as well as homicides, psychiatrists in leadership positions state that there is no silver bullet to resolve these problems. This is true to a certain degree, since they are looking for one mind-altering silver bullet pill. I explain to people that the Lone Ranger did not have just one silver bullet, but a belt of silver bullets, which I depict as a variety integrative treatment modalities to help individuals overcome whatever mental health issues they have to address.

THE BAD

A *bad* mental health professional doesn't hurt their patients but doesn't really care about them. I have seen this type person in various environments, especially in social service agencies and mental health facilities. For example, during a combat stress conference the chief psychiatrist from the Army gave a presentation—throughout his presentation he never referred to a person as an individual, patient, soldier, sailor, Marine, airman etc.; every time he referred to a person that he or someone else was working with he called them a "subject."

Other examples of bad psychiatrists I have experienced include people who primarily review records and give inappropriate advice to the counselors who are actually working with their clients. I recall a social service agency in California that had a chief psychiatrist making the recommendation that all prison inmates should be given psychiatric medication to make them more appropriate to be released into society. I've seen college faculty teach classes that they were not trained to teach in the field of mental health. Also, there are psychiatrists primarily concerned about making money who subsequently provide expedient treatment, such as prescribing psychiatric medications instead of providing talk therapy, which they are aware would be more effective but generate less revenue.

I recall a private patient I was seeing for therapy who was doing very well. This patient stated that her daughter would be returning from college for the semester break. She asked if I could see her daughter for the month that she would be home. I agreed. The first session with her daughter was productive and my overall prognosis was that she would only need to be seen for a few more sessions before returning to college with a plan on to how she could continue to make better life choices. She told me that at the very beginning of her first semester as a freshman, she was seeing a psychiatrist for psychotherapy. After the first session, the psychiatrist told her that she had a problem that would require her be seen by him once a week for the full four years she would be in college. This was obviously not the case since this patient was very pleased with the brief therapy she received and now had a specific way of dealing with her problems that did not require further therapy.

In a March 17, 2011 New York Times Newspaper article by reporter Gardiner Harris titled "New Efficiencies Taking Toll On Psychiatry-Talk Therapy No Longer Pays," the psychiatrist he interviewed generally stated that even though he knows talk therapy is effective, he can't delve into patients' problems, as his limited appointment time (approximately ten minutes) is just long enough to prescribe medication and nothing more. If a patient wants therapy, they must see a psychologist or social worker.[107]

The Pulitzer Prize award-winning play "Next to Normal" is a prime example of the above mentality. The mother in the play was seeing a psychiatrist as a result of a tragic family situation. The psychiatrist prescribed several medications, which led to even more problems in this woman's life. Throughout the course of the play, she realized how destructive these medications were and moved away from the psychiatrist and the medications, eventually developing a better relationship with her family and life in general.

---

107 Harris, G. (2011, March 5). Talk Doesn't Pay, So Psychiatry Turns Instead to Drug Therapy. Retrieved November 6, 2015, from http://www.nytimes.com/2011/03/06/health/policy/06doctors.html?pagewanted=3&_r=0&ref=health

THE UGLY

As mentioned above, the category of "the ugly" applies to psychiatrists, or any other mental health provider, who hurt their clients or patients. An example that I personally observed was when I was seeing a female patient for the very first time. When I greeted her and invited her to take a seat in my office, she immediately started crying uncontrollably. After calming her down, she revealed that since my last name started with the letter B, the association triggered an experience she recently had with a psychiatrist who was also called Dr. B. Upon further disclosure, the patient stated that this person sexually abused her. It's not unusual for psychiatrists or any other mental health professionals to lose their license for this totally inappropriate behavior.

As awful as this situation was, there are even worse situations where patients actually die from adverse reactions to psychiatric medications. Dr. Fred Bauman, a retired child neurologist in San Diego, has spent years researching the number of deaths in the military from psychiatric medication cocktails. He calls this dead-in-bed syndrome.

Dr. Bauman also advocates against other uses of psychiatric medications; for example, he argues that children should not receive amphetamines, such as Ritalin, for what he stated directly to me at a conference is "inappropriately diagnosed" ADD and ADHD. Without reservation, I would say Dr. Bauman is to be classified as a good physician. The evil/ugly physicians in the mental health field are the people who are doing just the opposite of what this prominent neurologist is doing and advocating.

The worst evil that I have seen in the field of mental health has been with psychiatrists who are in leadership positions advocating for large amounts of psychiatric medications being given to our vets, both at home and in the battlefield.

I recall in the 1970s, at a meeting held in San Diego, California for all military psychiatrists and psychologists, the chief psychiatrist made shocking comments. At this meeting, the chief Army psychiatrist stated clearly that, due to the advances in cognitive therapy being provided by psychologists, social workers, and marriage family counselors, the insurance companies were more receptive to short-term psychotherapy and less receptive to the long-term Freudian-type psychoanalysis that psychiatrists were providing. As a result, unless psychiatry could come up with a quick, cost-effective solution, they would soon go out of business as a profession. It appeared that during the '70s the pharmaceutical companies became aware of psychiatry's situation and, based on my perceptions, significant increases in psychiatric medications came to their aid. The result was a close relationship between the pharmaceutical companies and psychiatry to increase the prescriptions of psychiatric medications.

Today, the majority of psychiatrists prescribe psychiatric medication instead of providing any type of psychotherapy. As I mentioned earlier in the book, my experience and conversations with VA psychiatrists has been that they provide medications to the majority of patients they see who are diagnosed with PTSD.

It was estimated by the Citizens Commission on Human Rights International (CCHR) organization that psychiatry, in conjunction with Big Pharma, generates one third of a trillion dollars a year in fees and medication costs. In 2014, CCHR released an exceptional documentary called "Hidden Enemy," which is a must-view for anyone with questions about this subject.

I also read a shocking article by Kelli Kennedy, in which she states, "Medicare has stopped reimbursing a Miami doctor who prescribed about 96,685 mental health drugs to Medicaid patients in 18 months. According to state records, Dr. Fernando Mendez Villamil wrote an average of 153 prescriptions to adults and children every day between 2007 and 2009. That figure is nearly twice the number of the second highest prescriber on the list, who wrote 53,018 prescriptions over the same time period."[108]

What is most appalling to me is that a very small number of military psychiatrists convinced the Department of Defense (DoD) that they should allow our troops to receive psychiatric medications, not only while at home, but also on the battlefield. This advice was taken wholeheartedly, despite the fact that, as I mentioned in the congressional hearings of 2010, I observed a direct correlation between increased psychiatric medications in the military and increases in suicide. Where once soldiers were not allowed to be deployed if they were on psychiatric medications, now they are deployed with a 180-day supply. Social workers, medics, and others with multiple deployments stated openly

---

108   CCHR International. (n.d.). Retrieved November 21, 2015, from http://www.cchrint.org/2009/12/17/florida-psychiatrist-153-prescriptions-per-day-under-fed-invest/

at the combat stress conference that they feel approximately 90% of our troops used a psychiatric medication at some point while deployed.

As indicated, a medical health professional can lose his/her license for inappropriate behavior with a client, but there has been nothing done publicly to psychiatrists responsible for the drugging of our military. I see this mass drugging as criminal and malpractice. When a person is given multiple psychiatric medications and has an adverse reaction resulting in death, it's startling that criminal charges and dismissal from the military does not take place. This is *ugly*!

One can understand, by looking at my prior education and experiences, why I had a very strong leaning away from psychiatric medications and toward integrative treatment with the core of the treatment being Reality Therapy. In my master's program, I was required to take Medical Aspects courses at then called Allied Services for the Handicapped in Scranton Pennsylvania. At that time, Allied Services was a regional rehabilitation center where individuals from throughout Northeastern Pennsylvania were referred for rehabilitation services. It was a premier treatment facility where patients were seen for the various therapies and were also able to work in a sheltered vocational workshop on the grounds. While training there, I observed no psychiatric medications being prescribed. The families of the patients were also allowed to stay in cottages around the facility as part of the patient support program. At Allied, all the major community agencies were housed in this one facility. The Allied Services program was considered, at that time, one of the best in the United States.

Also, while in my two-year master's program, I did an internship in Binghamton New York. Through this internship I was exposed to psychiatrists working at the local mental hospital. When talking with psychiatrists, it was very clear that they were prescribing extensive psychiatric medications to their patients. When I tried to discuss specific counseling and therapy techniques, they focused more on medications. To this day, this initial contact with psychiatry has me doubtful as to the general profession's effectiveness, although I do have a great deal of respect for individual psychiatrists from whom I've learned much throughout my 48 years in the field. Primarily these psychiatrists I respected were focused on talk therapy and other integrative approaches that did not use psychiatric medications.

After arriving in California in the 1969 I attended grand rounds at the University Of San Francisco's (UCSF) teaching hospital. I had the opportunity to interact with many psychiatrists who worked there at the medical school. They practiced Freudian Psychoanalysis, as well as prescribed psychiatric medication. In the early '70s I was practicing Reality Therapy (RT) as my primary treatment modality and psychiatrists at UCSF frowned upon this approach. RT appeared to be a threat to them, even though the founder of RT was a psychiatrist. Later in my career I discovered why RT was a treatment modality they did not approve of: it was successful short-term therapy and could be administered by someone without a doctoral degree.

My first job in California was at Mendocino State Hospital in Ukiah. This allowed me to practice what I had learned from my previous college and graduate work, as well as my experiences at Allied Services. While working there, I discovered that it was nearly impossible to administer cognitive therapy (talk therapy) to medicated patients. The greatest success I had at Mendocino was with patients who were in treatment programs that did not utilize psychiatric medications.

While at Mendocino State Hospital, I had many previously homeless veterans as patients. They had been living on the streets of San Francisco and were picked up and legally taken to the hospital for help. The hospital gave them an opportunity to become physically healthy for the first time in many months—in some cases years. With a healthy body and a mind clear of street drugs and alcohol, they had a chance to work on their future.

There were various treatment programs at the hospital, each housed in its own building. In addition to their individual treatment unit program therapy, many veterans from these different treatment program units attended a transitional rehabilitation group therapy program that I developed. The focus of the group was on leaving the hospital and preparing for a job, vocational training, and a healthy living environment, which for many was a therapeutic community halfway house. They were accepted, while in the hospital, into the hospital-based California Department of Rehabilitation program, which provided them with a counselor, job training, schooling, work clothing, and work tools if necessary. A job placement specialist also worked with their vocational counselor. The therapy group worked so well that it was written up in a journal and used by the Department Of Rehabilitation staff statewide. This program not only changed many people's lives, but also saved their life.

REALITY THERAPY/CHOICE THEORY PSYCHOLOGY AS MY TREATMENT OF CHOICE AND THE CORE OF INTEGRATED WELLNESS PROGRAMS

Dr. William Glasser, the founder of Reality Therapy, often stated in his workshops that his concepts are an outgrowth of his mentor's way of treating patients. He referred throughout his career to Dr. Harrington as his mentor, from whom he got the idea of Reality Therapy.

One of Dr. Glasser's first positions was at the Veterans Administration Hospital in Los Angeles, which was a facility used as a teaching hospital by UCLA medical school. His wife, Naomi, in the 1970s, explained to me that Bill was hired as clinical faculty to supervise psychiatry residents. Dr. Glasser taught his residents Reality Therapy, which they utilized in working with patients, including those who were diagnosed as psychotic. Dr. Glasser never used psychiatric medications, nor did he teach his residents to use psychiatric medications in working with their patients. Although clinical faculty at a teaching hospital is a non-paid position, Dr. Glasser was very diligent in teaching his residents his philosophy of treatment that he learned from Dr. Harrington. Over the course of his first year as clinical faculty, his residents were more successful in working with their patients than the other residents who were supervised by permanent paid faculty. Dr. Glasser's residents had the lowest rate of recidivism in the department. Dr. Glasser was not invited back as clinical faculty the following year.

Dr. Glasser's next position was as a psychiatric consultant at the Ventura School for Girls, a youth authority facility. This is where Dr. Glasser developed his concept of Reality Therapy and taught it throughout the facility. The results were astonishing; the recidivism rate at the facility dropped significantly while Dr. Glasser was employed. As a result, Dr. Glasser wrote his book *Reality Therapy.*

According to Naomi, the director of Ventura School for Girls received a call from the psychiatry faculty at UCLA requesting that the school dismiss Dr. Glasser because of his unusual approach to psychotherapy. The school director ignored the suggestion, stating that his staff and the residents of the school had never done better. This was the beginning of what is now called Reality Therapy/Choice Theory Psychology, which has grown throughout the world with thousands of therapists, internationally, being certified as reality therapists. Dr. Glasser has written approximately 30 textbooks on how to apply RT/CT in every aspect of society, including mental health clinics, schools, private business (management), etc. In order to get an in-depth understanding of RT/CT, I suggest reading some of Dr. Glasser's published textbooks. For the purpose of giving an over-all understanding of RT/CT, I will discuss what most appealed to me with this approach.

In 1970 I read the book *Reality Therapy* and was immediately impressed that it presented many of the exact things I was doing with people whom I was seeing for counseling. My first impression was that Reality Therapy was easy to understand but I found out as time went on, it was harder to apply than traditional psychoanalysis. As has been my practice, I contacted the Reality Therapy Institute in 1970 and asked if I could meet Dr. Glasser and attend his workshops. I proceeded to take three one-week workshops over a period of one and a half years, with continuous supervision throughout. During the third and final workshop, I had to demonstrate, one-on-one, with Dr. Glasser, that I knew and could practice, as well as teach, Reality Therapy. Dr. Bill Glasser remained my mentor for over forty years until his passing in 2014.

I can honestly say that every time I spoke with Dr. Glasser, I learned something new; that is because he was always learning something new. To illustrate this point, about five years before he passed he asked me if he could be a student in a workshop I was teaching on the HARRT program. To have my mentor as a student was one of the highlights of my career. He sat in the front row and asked more questions than anyone in the room.

I have taken classes over the years from some very prominent icons in the fields of psychology, psychiatry, marriage family therapy, and psychodrama, and I've learned that RT/CT is the most effective approach for the work I do. RT/CT is effective for me because it teaches a client or patient to live in the present. In other words, dealing with the here and now since there is nothing one can do to go back and change the past. Traditional psychoanalysis spends many hours discussing the whys and past behaviors before ever getting to the point of "What are you going to do now?" RT/CT discusses the past briefly but does not dwell on it. The focus is on choices that an individual needs to make today to move forward. RT/CT teaches people to assume responsibility for their behavior and helps them make better choices to achieve their goals.

Involvement is the key ingredient in practicing RT/CT. The formula that I have come up with over the years that best describes RT/CT is $I + C = T$. That is to say, involvement (I) plus caring (C) equals trust (T) when working with any individual. The idea of therapist involvement was a departure from traditional therapy methods that I learned in graduate school. Involvement requires the therapist to not only learn about their client's life, but also to share information about their own life, which allows the patient to see their therapist as an equal. It also allows the patient to determine whether a therapist is a good fit based on their own life experiences. This empowers the patient by giving them immediate responsibility and control over their experience.

As mentioned in a previous chapter, there are levels of involvement that the therapist always remembers. The level of involvement appropriate between the therapist and a client/patient is always kept in mind. By demonstrating you care about the individual, you are working with them to achieve their goals and demonstrating a concern for their well-being. This leads to trust, which is the most important ingredient in any relationship.

RT/CT states that all human beings have basic and higher level psychological needs that they strive to meet every day in their life. The basic need for survival (food, clothing, shelter, and sex) and the higher psychological needs of love/belonging, power/achievement, fun/enjoyment, and freedom are inherent in all people unless they have a genetic defect. From the moment one is born, they strive to meet these needs and when they do, they put a picture of the need-fulfilling situation in their brains. Dr. Glasser called this internal photo album the "quality world." This album builds as one continues through life in an attempt to meet their psychological needs. If one does not meet their psychological needs in a healthy manner, it creates psychological pain, which often results decreasingly unhealthy attempts to meet those needs. This explains why some people turn to meeting their involvement needs by joining gangs and utilizing drugs.

In the military, soldiers meet their need for involvement and love more intensely than they ever could in the civilian world. They actually count on their peers to meet their need for survival, and the intense love and belonging follows. This is the reason many soldiers choose to perform multiple tours. This need for involvement with others is the most powerful of all needs for a human being. Many times people get independence and dependence reversed. People are proud to say they are *independent* and they don't need anyone but themselves. But a truly independent person is one who has a lot of people and things in their lives. This interdependence allows one to have many alternatives in their lives, therefore if they lose one thing or person, they can move on. Being dependent is only having yourself or very few other things in life to depend upon.

The best example of this need for interdependence is when we had two patients at the hospital and coincidentally they had the same impairment. They were both paraplegics and also both were college professors. One was, as the staff saw it, independent—not needing anyone before the accident and taking care of his needs with no help. The other was married and had a large family. During this person's hospital stay, his family was always there helping him throughout the rehabilitation process. The so-called independent patient did not need anybody and took care of his own needs in the hospital. I tried to explain to the physical therapist that the person they saw as being helpless and needing his family support was going to do better once leaving the hospital than the patient they saw as being independent. It was very difficult for the therapist to understand what I was saying. Although I did not directly work with either patient, I followed their progress once they were released from the hospital. The patient who had extended family returned to his university as a professor. The other patient who was seen as independent never returned fully to his job and eventually committed suicide.

As you can see, it is extremely important to have many people and things in your life to depend on to be truly independent. Therefore, a soldier is independent because he depends on other soldiers within his squad and platoon, NCOs, and commanding officers. He not only depends on them but also needs them in his life to stay alive.

When deployed, the soldier also meets their need for power/achievement more intensely than they could ever meet it in the civilian world. By slightly moving a finger they can initiate an action that would destroy a building. Moving the throttle of an airplane can move a soldier to a space in the sky with the blink of an eye.

The need for fun and freedom is also intensely present on the battlefield. Fun can be seen as learning new information; this is quite evident in military training and even more so in combat. Therefore, when using RT/CT in therapy with a veteran, it is imperative to teach the veteran about their psychological needs, including how they met them in combat and how they can meet them when returning to civilian life. They need to understand that the needs will not be met as intensely as in combat but can still be met in a fashion that will make the transition from the battlefield back to the neighborhood easier.

In an effort to meet these needs, many veterans turn to drugs. However, drugs actually give one the false feeling of meeting all of their needs intensely. Since this is a passive pleasure, it does not last and, if continued, becomes very destructive.

To understand how one makes good choices, you need to understand Choice Theory Psychology. We can use the analogy of a front-wheel drive automobile. The engine of this automobile propels the car, but the driver determines the direction of the car. When the driver steers, the front wheels turn in response to his or her actions. Meanwhile, the rear wheels literally and figuratively go along for the ride. Likewise, our psychological needs are like the engine; they propel us through life, but it is ultimately what we decide to do and think that determines the direction our life takes. Our decisions and actions are those front wheels that steer us through life in positive or negative directions; as a result of those thoughts and actions, our feelings and physiology (the rear wheels) follow along, and they determine how we feel both mentally and physically.

When we are feeling bad, it means that what we are thinking and doing isn't sufficiently meeting our psychological needs. Therefore it's important to ask what we need to do differently. If a person is having trouble making better choices on their own, talking to a trusted professional can help.

One of the tools that I use with people is to teach them alternative thinking to make appropriate choices—an RT/CT essential in therapy. When a person is seeing me in my office, it would not be unusual to ask him/her/them to give me four different ways that he/she/they could get home from my office. I would also assign homework that requires them to come up with four different ways of doing certain things throughout the day. For example, they could come up with four different ways they could have dinner that evening. They could go to their friend's house for dinner, stop at a fast food restaurant, go to the grocery store and buy ingredients for dinner to cook, or ask a spouse to bring dinner home.

The point is to develop alternative thinking patterns and recognize that there are always options to choose from. As the old saying goes, *there's more than one way to skin a cat*, but many people get used to knowing only one way. If a person develops an alternative thinking habit, it becomes like a scanner on a radio that stops on the strongest signal. A person's brain becomes a scanner of choices to make and usually stops on the most appropriate choice.

Reality Therapy/Choice Theory Psychology works since integrative wellness treatment involves choosing various appropriate treatment modalities. It boils down to making the correct choice of the specific treatment modalities available (i.e. peer counseling, exercise, yoga, nutrition counseling, etc.) that will match with what the individual is striving to achieve. An Individual Wellness Program (IWP) is a process where you look at how an individual is meeting all of their psychological and physical needs now and how together you can come up with other choices that will lead them to where they eventually want to be.

It is important for any effective therapeutic approach to be easy to understand. You don't need a PhD or MD to understand Reality Therapy/Choice Theory Psychology. When I taught workshops in RT/CT, it wasn't unusual for people with a high school degree to do better than highly credentialed psychiatrists and psychologists in getting the concept and practicing the counseling techniques.

Although RT/CT is easy to understand, it took quite a bit of work to practice—unlike traditional psychoanalysis, which is difficult to understand but easy to practice and stories are told of the psychoanalyst falling asleep during a session. The accessibility of RT/CT for people with all levels of education is one of the reasons Dr. Glasser received so much criticism from the field of psychiatry. His approach, which was more effective than what they were doing, was a thorn in their side and profession. That may be the reason he wrote one of his books titled *CAUTION: Psychiatry May Be Hazardous to Your Mental Health*. In this book he describes the inordinate amount of brain-altering psychiatric medications psychiatrists administer in place of real caring and involved talk therapy.

When describing RT/CT, one can see how it is the core of many of the integrative treatment modalities discussed. It's like a multi-strand rope that is wound over a steel core for strength. Whether your program involves exercise, group counseling, music therapy, dance therapy, yoga, etc., if you look hard, the concepts of RT/CT are there.

For example, let's look at dance therapy and ask the following questions:

- Why is it that people have improvement in physical and mental health through dance?

- Why do people who are depressed, to the extreme of thinking about suicide, now feel empowered and move on constructively with their life?

- Why do people stop using drugs when they see *Falling Star*, the dance movie? The movie is a short film with only dance and no dialogue. In twelve different scenes it shows the demise of a young man who becomes addicted to drugs. He loses his friends and eventually his life. There were numerous letters and personal comments from people who actually stopped using drugs and changed destructive behavior after viewing the dance movie or taking regular dance classes.

- Why do dancers work practically for free just to dance?

- What innate feelings drive very young children to want to dance?

- Why do people dance to celebrate and dance when they are sad (i.e. as in some funeral processions)?

- Why do people dance prior to going into war or when they celebrate peace? At one of the combat stress conferences I direct, tough Marines who saw the dance movie "Fallen Star" or observed a dance show at the conference, stated they wanted to learn how to dance.

- How can dance be part of an integrative treatment program for combat stress?

- Why do soldiers in a war zone, on their resting time, (and even POWs in captivity) dance with each other?

Some answers:

Physically, when dancing, people burn calories, improve heart function, build new neurological pathways in the brain[109] that improve thought process, release the body's natural chem-

---

109 Glasser, W. (1976). *Positive addiction. New York: Harper & Row.*

icals (endorphins, adrenaline) that are associated with positive feelings and drives..

Psychologically, people who dance meet higher human genetic needs per Glasser's Choice Theory Psychology, including:

Love/Involvement — You become emotionally close and physically close to the people you dance with. A strong bond is established, even with new people in a dance class or group. You are physically close and touch the person you dance with in a socially acceptable way that cannot be done in almost any other social setting. You are allowed into each other's personal space, even if you are not a relative or close friend. For the moment, you are treated as if you are very close and involved in a meaningful friendship with your partner.

Power/Achievement — You are in control of your body. You see yourself in a new light, being able to move with music (music is also therapeutic, and dance always is associated with music). You feel strong both mentally and physically. The clothes you wear tell people you are fit—a dancer. A special skill is developing within you—a sense of power is apparent in how you feel and your sense of your own changing physiology. People respect you for your dedication. People watch you and non-dancers comment your new skill; even if it is not great, it's better than what it was prior to this endeavor.

Fun — Whenever you can move freely and be in unison with others, it is need-fulfilling fun; even alone you feel that you have no cares when you are moving (reciprocal inhibition). You are releasing endorphins while expressing emotions in a positive way, which gives a physical sense of well-being in and of itself. You are learning something new that involves your total body and mind. When you learn something new and are able to demonstrate the new skill it is seen as being fun.

Freedom — You are free to create your own style on a dance floor. You are a unique person, as is every human being, and your dance style is yours alone. Your fingerprint can be seen by what you project from your body and expression. Ballet, lyrical jazz, modern dance etc. are all about expression of self. Dance provides total freedom to do as you like. You are free to touch others mentally and physically. Free to elevate your spirit and sole. Free to express yourself (this was one of the ways POWs, while in captivity, met this need for freedom.)

So as you can see, something as simple as dance can be quite need fulfilling and lead to physical and emotional strength that can move a person through hard times. I remember one member of a dance company telling me that the only time she felt truly happy when was when she was dancing. When I asked her why, she said she had terminal brain cancer and when dancing, she was in a state of mind and body where she was not thinking about her problem and thoroughly enjoying herself.

INTEGRATIVE TREATMENT RECOMMENDATIONS MADE TO VETS AT MY RESTAURANT

For many years, I have been providing counseling and psychotherapy in a wide variety of environments including mental health hospitals, clinics, drug treatment programs, halfway houses, military bases, military hospitals, outdoors, etc., but my most unique experience has been as the owner of a restaurant/bar.

In 2009 I invested in a restaurant/bar to help a friend expand his business. Within ten months my partner had financial problems and left me as the sole owner. The last thing I wanted at this point in my life was to own a restaurant/bar. To try to make the best out of that situation, I developed a relationship with a nearby military base to provide catering for events on base that various military units were having. I catered several events for individual military units, as well as a large (500-person) event for the secretary of labor, who was developing a program on base to train Marines on civilian jobs prior to their discharge. Over time, word got out on the base, as well as in a local newspaper article, that I specialized in dealing with the residual effects of combat stress. Before I knew it, many of the active-duty military personnel would stop by the restaurant to talk with me about their concerns and symptoms.

What initially turned out to be a bad investment gone sour now turned into a very positive experience for my veteran customers and me. Over a beer and some food, many veterans felt very comfortable discussing issues that they did not want to discuss on base. Obviously, this was not formal therapy that the individuals paid for, but a friendly conversation with another veteran who showed concern for their well-being. For example, I had three Marine aviators stop by to talk about their concerns about injuring civilians when they were dropping their ordinance. I asked them if this conversation came up back at their base with their commanding officer and other aviators. They stated that they were hesitant to discuss this issue on base because it could interfere with their flight status. In the amount of time it took them to drink a draft beer and eat a meal, they felt comfortable with the end result of our conversation.

I recall one veteran who was a patient at the nearby Veterans Administration Hospital. I spoke with him several times at the restaurant; he enjoyed coming in to choose from the twenty craft beer taps. He never revealed having any problems until he was comfortable enough to bring another veteran with him to discuss his issue that resulted from combat. He explained that the psychiatrist at the VA diagnosed him with PTSD due to an abnormal red blood cell count. He stated they could not figure out any other reason for his blood count other than post-traumatic stress disorder for which they prescribed psychiatric medications. I explained that this diagnosis was not consistent with an abnormal CBC. After a conversation with this young veteran, I recommended that he see a physician who specializes with identifying blood parasites. I saw this veteran a few weeks later and he expressed his gratitude—a blood parasite had been discovered.

These are just a few examples of conversations held at the restaurant. The restaurant in a sense, became a clinic, NCO/O club, and family support haven where I was able to talk on the average with at least one active or retired veteran (ranging from WWII to present) every couple of days. There were times when officer's call was held at the restaurant, immediately followed by the officer's families coming in afterwards. There were promotion parties where I was the unofficial CO, ensuring that nothing got out of hand. When various military units could not afford a complete food menu for Christmas parties, I was fortunate enough to be in a position where I could donate food for the occasion. Overall, of all the awards I received while in the military, the plaques given to me by the Marines for helping them out was deeply appreciated.

CHAPTER 8

HUMAN ASSISTANCE RAPID RESPONSE TEAM (HARRT) PROGRAM

For complete instructions as to how to administer the HARRT program and to download the total protocol, please visit the book website at: www.bartpbillings.com

During the first Persian Gulf War, many units were deployed on short notice. When this occurred, immediate human services to personnel and their families were lacking, resulting in unresolved conflicts for staff being sent off to their new duty stations. There were situations where personnel became casualties of the stress resulting from unresolved family, personal, financial, job, issues not being resolved prior to deployment. As a result, some staff were prematurely returned from duty while others were negatively affected when returning from their deployment. Also, some soldiers were distracted while on duty due to bad news from home that should have been resolved before deployment.

Many problems could have been avoided with professional assistance for doing solid pre-planning prior to deployment. It would allow the soldier time to pre-plan all alternatives that could be followed by their family and employer once they are deployed and no longer available.

During the initial Persian Gulf War, I was the commanding officer of an Army Reserve general hospital section that was called to active duty. The hospital staff did not go to active duty as one complete unit, but were deployed every few weeks to different locations throughout the world. Their deployment was for a year, requiring them on very short notice to leave their families, employers, and community, all without knowing their final assignment.

One of my duties was to have a total hospital formation and call out the names of the soldiers who were then required to get on a bus and be transported to the higher headquarters for final deployment. This type of experience occurred three separate times before the total unit was deployed. It was very traumatic for the soldiers being deployed, as well as their families, who were watching through a chain-link fence.

When the hospital soldiers returned from their one-year deployment, there were many problems they experienced as a result of being deployed on such a short notice.

Many of the soldiers in the unit said that the Army had no heart in the way it prepared people for either deployment or returning home. At that time I talked with some of my staff and decided we would institute a yearly workshop and figure out a way to improve this situation for the future. What resulted was the Human Assistance Rapid Response Team (HARRT). In a sense, we gave the Army a HARRT. The program covered questions pertaining to all aspects of a person's life, such as:

1. Medical

2. Family/Support

3. Vocational

4. Social

5. Economic

6. Legal

7. Spiritual

8. Psychological

Since I had previously developed the HARRT questionnaire concept in my private practice to determine patients' readiness to enter employment, go off to school, etc., it made sense to apply the program to my military unit. One must realize that one of the keys in this questionnaire being successfully used is the interaction of the person asking the questions and the participant.

It should be understood that the person administering the questions should have some minimal training on how to administer the questionnaire, especially for the questions related to psychological needs. This questionnaire should not be given to individuals taking it on their own or in a group.

Start of questionnaire:

INTERVIEW FORM SUMMARY

The purpose of this interview is to discuss safety and security issues during peacetime and wartime for you and your family. If there is information discovered in the interview that may affect your deployment (or otherwise), it may be brought to the attention of the commander for his/her discretion. Put '"X" in blanks if a problem or potential problems exists. The left blank is for the interviewee and the right blank is for family members. Indicate "OK" if no follow-up needed.

SUMMARY PAGE

This summary page is to be kept by commander and a copy is to be given to soldier. Note: To the left of each item place an "I" for the person answering questionnaire and an "F" when the person is answering questions for a family member. Only general statements are made on the summary page with no details. It should only show what areas need to be improved upon and what areas are ok. Basically a go/no go indicator for the commander to determine readiness for deployment.

I'| F' Interviewee's Name _____

Date _____

1. Medical
2. Family/Support
3. Vocational

4. Social
5. Economic
6. Legal
7. Spiritual

Addresses the psychological needs of the individual or family member, how those needs are currently being met, and how they will be met on active duty.

1. Belonging /Involvement
2. Power/ Achievement/Self Worth   .
3. Freedom
4. Fun
5. Survival

Are there any other concerns that you may have at this time?

_____

Action that needs to be taken:

_____

Note: Is there a Family Care Plan attached? Please check either "Yes" or "No."

[__ Yes] [__ No]

_____

Interviewer - Print Name / Rank

_____

Interviewee Print Name/Rank

HARRT⁽ᴿ⁾ QUESTIONNAIRE:

INTERVIEW FORM

Interviewee's Name _____

Date _____

MEDICAL

I / F

1. Have you ever been hospitalized?

(a) Yes - How many times? _____

(b) For what reasons? _____

_____

_____

_____

2. Are you currently taking medication(s)?

(a) Yes-Type? _____

(b) Purpose? For what reason?

_____

_____

3. Medical conditions precluding mobilization?

_____

_____

4. Do you have a current profile?

_____

_____

5. **How would you rate your health?**

   ☐ Good   ☐ Fair   ☐ Poor

   _____ _____

   _____

   _____

6. **Are you currently under the care of a doctor / physician?**

(a) Yes - What reason?

   _____

   _____

(b) How long?_____

7. **Do you have any known allergies?**

   _____

   _____

   _____

8. **Have you been seen for counseling or therapy in the past?**

   _____

   _____

   _____

9. **Has anyone ever told you that you may have an alcohol / drug problem?**

   _____

   _____

   _____

10. Is your immunization up to date? Last physical
    exam (civilian and military)

_____

FAMILY SUPPORT

1. Describe your current living situation.

_____

_____

_____

2. Whom do you turn to for emotional support?

_____

3. How do you feel about being in the military?

_____

4. How do you feel that you will cope if activated for a
    significant period of time?

_____

VOCATIONAL

1. What is your current job? Military? / As a civilian?

_____

_____

2. Do you like your job? In the military? / As a civilian?

(a) Yes

(b) No – Why? Explain.

_____

_____

(c) What are you doing to change the situation?

_____

_____

3. How would your employer feel about you being mobilized?

_____

4. Do you feel competent performing your military MOS?

_____

5. Do you have job-related or specialty skills that are not being utilized?

_____

SOCIAL

1. What do you do for fun / recreation?

_____

_____

_____

2. Do you have friends?

_____

3. Do you consider yourself a loner?

_____

_____

_____

4. Do you find it easy to make friends?
   ___ YES ___ NO

5. How would your social network be affected by your leaving?

_____

_____

_____

6. What type of recreational activities can you be involved in while on active duty?

_____

_____

_____

7. How do you use your spare time?

_____

_____

_____

ECONOMIC

1. Do you have any current financial commitments you would have difficulty paying if called for active duty?

_____

_____

_____

2. **Do you have any current financial matters that you consider to be a problem?**

    _____

3. **Who currently pays your bills?**

    _____

    _____

    _____

    If self, who can take over this responsibility?

    _____

    _____

4. **Is designee capable of managing your finances?**

    _____

    _____

    _____

5. **Do you have at least $1,000 in the bank? _____ Checking? / Saving?**

6. **Does your family have access to your bank accounts?**

    _____

LEGAL

1. **Do you have a will / power of attorney currently in place? If so, are you satisfied with it?**

    _____

    _____

    _____

2. Do you have any legal actions pending?

_____

_____

_____

3. Do you need to use the Soldier / Sailors Relief Act?

_____

4. Do you have a power of attorney for health care? Designee?

_____

5. Do you have a passport?

_____

6. Regarding your vital papers, do you know their location or currently have them in your possession? These include but are not limited to: marriage certificate, birth certificate, divorce papers, passport, immunization record, and INS papers.

_____

7. Do you feel you need an attorney assigned to you?

_____

SPIRITUAL

1. How do you meet your spiritual needs?

_____

_____

_____

2. What is your religion?

    _____

3. Do you currently practice a religion?

    _____

4. Do you plan to attend church if mobilized?

    _____

5. Do you need any special consideration to practice /
    meet your spiritual needs?

    _____

    _____

    _____

6. Do you need to see a chaplain prior to being mobi-
    lized?

_____

PSYCHOLOGICAL NEEDS

Select an appropriate number that best rates the strength of perceived need at the present time. Place "I" for individual OR "F"
for family member in the 1-5 rating blanks.

1. **Belonging / Involvement**
    LOW ____1 ___2 ____3 ___4 ___5 HIGH

a) How many close friends do you have?
    (Army / Civilian) _____

b) Do you have a spouse / significant other or children?
    ___ YES ___ NO

c) Are you involved with other people in after-work activities? ___ YES ___ NO

d) Do you consider yourself a satisfied individual? ___ YES ___ NO

e) Do you find it easy to make friends? ___ YES ___ NO

f) Do you have a pet? ___ YES ___ NO

g) Do you belong to any fraternity / sorority clubs / social clubs? ___ YES ___ NO

2. **Power / Self Worth**
   LOW ___1 ___2 ___3 ___4 ___5 HIGH

a) Are you employed? ___ YES ___ NO

b) Do people respect your opinion? ___ YES ___ NO

c) Are you satisfied with your job in the military? In the civilian work place? ___ YES ___ NO

d) Do you consider yourself a leader? ___ YES ___ NO

e) What is your most recent accomplishment / achievement?

   _____

   _____

   _____

3. **Freedom**
   LOW ___1 ___2 ___3 ___4 ___5 HIGH

a) Do you feel you have choices you can make in your military / civilian career life? ___ YES ___ NO

b) Do you feel you have a choice to stay in the military?
___ YES ___ NO

c) Do you feel you can speak your opinion to your NCO / CO? ___ YES ___ NO

d) Do you make good choices? ___ YES ___ NO

4. Fun

LOW ____1 ___2 ____3 ___4 ___5 HIGH

a) What do you do for recreational activities?
__ Play sports
__ Music
__ Read
__ Go to movies
__ Drink
__ Other (Please specify)

_____

_____

b) What type of leisure activities would you engage in while on active duty?

_____

_____

_____

c) Have your recreational activities ever interfered with your job? ___ YES ___ NO

d) What makes you laugh?

_____

_____

5. **Survival**

LOW ____1 ___2 ____3 ___4 ___5 HIGH

a) Do you feel you are trained well enough to survive in the field? ___ YES ___ NO

b) Would your family have difficulty meeting their needs for food, clothing, and shelter when you are deployed? ___ YES ___ NO

c) Are there any family medical conditions or problems that would be affected when you are mobilized? ___ YES ___ NO

d) Do you feel your family will be in a safe living environment without you? ___ YES ___ NO

e) Do you feel you are mentally / psychologically fit for active duty? ___ YES ___ NO

f) Does your family have enough access to medical, exchange services, commissary, etc.? ___ YES ___ NO

g) Do you have enough money to buy what you need when deployed? ___ YES ___ NO

CHAPTER 9

TRANSITIONAL REACTIONS: MAKING THE TRANSITION FROM MILITARY TO CIVILIAN LIFE

B ased on my history and what I have learned in making my own transitions and helping others make transitions, I want to start this chapter with what I hope can be the future for helping veterans make successful transitions from military life to the civilian world.

I propose a military transition program that would consist of deploying a "transitional readiness team" to the combat zone two weeks prior to the unit's return to the States. The team, consisting of retired Special Operations veterans (who would immediately have face validity with returning combat troops) such as Navy SEALs, Army Green Berets, Air Force Para Rescue, and/or

Marine Recon veterans. This team would be specially trained in transitional mental health techniques to help the troops prepare for return to the United States, providing counseling, discussing normal reactions to combat, and identifying potential problem areas and how to resolve them.

The readiness team would also accompany the unit back to United States and work with individual platoon-size components for one hour every day for thirty days. During the hour of mandated mental health training (MT), which would occur after the troopers' mandated physical training (PT), all would be encouraged to talk about the reactions of troops returning home from combat. The readiness team would make the veterans aware of some of the most common symptoms they may experience and also provide training on how to overcome normal problems resulting from combat trauma and stress, such as dealing with nightmares, hypervigilance, depression, etc.

During the last week of the month-long transitional period, the focus would turn to the families of returning soldiers, with treatment staff providing information specifically directed at how family members can identify triggers of adverse behavior and how best to help the soldier work through these periods of stress. By the end of the thirty-day transitional period, any troops that have been observed as exhibiting suicidal or homicidal ideation would be referred to the appropriate mental health treatment program for continued counseling. The referring special ops team member would accompany the soldier to the follow-up treatment and be part of the treatment team throughout this extended program.

One of the key pieces of information the special ops team will provide returning troops is an explanation of what I call "transitional reactions." Whenever anyone makes a transition from one way of living to another, there is always stress involved. For example, when someone goes from high school to college there is a transitional reaction. The stress associated with this change is normal and an indication that your life is changing. If the associated stress is looked upon as not normal, there's a strong tendency to back off and not move forward. By making one aware of the normal stress associated with transitions, they are better able to prepare for and cope with the change.

In other words, if, when making a transition, you do not experience a degree of stress, then there's a strong possibility that either no significant change is taking place or denial is taking place. People should look forward to stress when making transitions as it indicates that they are growing and moving forward. This transitional reaction is quite common for military veterans when going from a training situation into combat. It's a normal healthy stress that lets you know life is about to change and you are prepared to deal with this change. The period of training a veteran experiences before going into combat is several months long. Therefore the period of training to deal with the transitional stress of coming from the battlefield to the civilian community should be no less important and the veteran should be allowed a significant period of time to learn how to make this stressful transition successfully. That should be done in a comfortable environment, without the use of brain-altering psychiatric drugs, where counseling and integrative treatment is the primary treatment modality.

PSYCHIATRIC MEDS ON THE BATTLEFIELD CAN INTERFERE WITH TRANSITIONS AFTER DEPLOYMENT

Not only are veterans being medicated when they return home, but some veterans are being given a 180-day supply of psychiatric medications while they are deployed. When I was once asked on a radio show how much psychiatric meds are dispensed to our troops on the battlefield, I replied that it is easier to determine how much cocaine is transported from Columbia to the United States. This is due to the fact that many individuals in combat areas are given psychiatric medications from several sources, including psychiatrists, medics, and other comrades in arms. One Marine whom I saw as a patient was given an antidepressant (in Iraq) by the medical staff when he requested something that he could use to stop smoking. He took this antidepressant throughout his deployment and when returning home, he stated that he was having an adverse reaction to this medication and proceeded to go to the hospital. At the hospital he explained the difficulties he was having to the medical staff; after reviewing his medical records from his deployment in Iraq, they stated there was no record of him ever being given any type of medication.

At one of our combat stress conferences, a social worker told me that while she was deployed in Iraq, the psychiatrist she worked with was prescribing so much medication that the pharmacist refused to fill his prescriptions. The psychiatrist went into the pharmacy facility, took boxes of drugs, put them in individual plastic bags, and handed them out to the troops. He stored these medications in the social workers' quarters and it wasn't until the social worker reported his inappropriate behavior that he was stopped. The same social worker explained that when she did a tour in Afghanistan, the commanding psychiatrist of her medical unit chastised her for being a social worker, stating that she was no good to him unless she could prescribe psychiatric medications.

As you can see, the extensive prescribing of psychiatric medications is tragic. We are taking a normal human being with a normal brain and medicating them; their brain is altered. Overall, it is very difficult to not only function on the battlefield when medicated, but to make the transition back to neighborhood and family when you are on brain-altering psychiatric medications.

RETURNING TO THE NEIGHBORHOOD

Four-Star General James N. Mattis gave a realistic viewpoint of what it's like when a veteran returns home, and his plea is clear: treat veterans with respect and gratitude for their service.

Rather than labeling them as "damaged ... or with disorders,"[110] he believes that these wartime experiences have the potential to shape the veteran into a person who has learned much through traumatic circumstances—and who can return home and make a contribution in civilian life as well.

David Zucchino and David Cloud describe a "warrior class" within the military, not unlike ancient Greek and Roman warriors who had difficulty integrating themselves into civilian life upon returning home from battle. To make matters worse, the number of people who have not served in the military and don't understand what a veteran experiences are growing. This means that veterans don't have a reliable support system when they return home. "While the U.S. waged a war in Vietnam 50 years ago with 2.7 million men conscripted from every segment of society, less than one-half of 1% of the U.S. population is in the armed services today — the lowest rate since World War II. America's recent wars are authorized by a U.S. Congress whose members have the lowest rate of military service in history, led by three successive commanders in chief that never served on active duty."[111]

The last decade of war has affected the relationship between our society and the military. The authors' state, "Gen. Martin Dempsey, chairman of the Joint Chiefs of Staff, wrote ... 'As a nation, we've learned to separate the warrior from the war. But

110 Mattis, James N. (2015, April 17). The Meaning of Their Service. *The Wall Street Journal*. *Retrieved from http://www.wsj.com/articles/the-meaning-of-their-service-1429310859*.
111 Zucchino, David and Cloud, David S. (2015, June 20). U.S. Military and Civilians Are Increasingly Divided. *Los Angeles Times. Retrieved from http://www.latimes.com/nation/ la-na-warrior-main-20150524-story.html#page=1*.

we still have much to learn about how to connect the warrior to the citizen.... We can't allow a sense of separation to grow between us.'"[112]

The importance for a workable transitional program is especially critical for veterans who do not make a career out of the military and do not receive retirement benefits. Since currently so many veterans are taken from the reserve and National Guard ranks, they return to their communities where many of them don't have access to military support services.

The veteran who spends twenty years or more in the military is in a much better position to make the transition to civilian life, since not only does he/she have financial retirement support but also social support. Retired veterans most often live near both other veterans and a military base, which provides various types of support, from medical services to shopping privileges. Even in retirement, this emerging warrior class is visible in the various locations throughout the United States.

Choice Theory Psychology states that one of the higher-level psychological needs we all have is the need for power/self-worth, and in our society this translates into meaningful employment. Career veterans meet this need by working in the military for twenty or more years. That is why it is especially important for a non-career veteran transitioning back to the community to have a solid plan on how to meet this need.

---

112 Zucchino, David and Cloud, David S. (2015, June 20). U.S. Military and Civilians Are Increasingly Divided. *Los Angeles Times. Retrieved from http://www.latimes.com/nation/ la-na-warrior-main-20150524-story.html#page=1*

One of the best transitional programs I have ever observed was in San Diego, California. The program is called Reboot, and it combines transitional counseling with practical preparation for vocations. I had the opportunity to be a keynote speaker at one of their graduations and was impressed with their training. During the graduation, all of their students were required to give a brief talk about what the program provided and the impact it made on their transition from the military to the civilian world. The students were very clear in what their future career goals were and how they were going to achieve these goals. Seeing the outcome of this program further confirmed my previous belief that either counseling or vocational training alone is not as effective as when both are occurring simultaneously.

My summary of what they have accomplished would not be enough to do them justice in explaining their outstanding work. I feel strongly that the Reboot program model should be implemented nationwide. Their success rate, in the 95th percentile, is astonishing. Find out how you can get help today. Call 866-535-7624 or visit REBOOT online at www.rebootworkshop. org.[113]

---

113   Reboot Workshop. (n.d.). Retrieved November 6, 2015, from http://www.nvtsi.org

CHAPTER 10

THE EVOLUTION OF THE TRI-SERVICE COMBAT STRESS CONFERENCE

For over twenty-two years, every May for five days, The International Military and Civilian Combat Stress Conference has covered topics ranging from the battlefield to the neighborhood. It was first called the Tri-Service Combat Stress Conference and was held at Camp Pendleton Naval Hospital. The conference was organized by the United States Army Reserve 6252, General Hospital, Section 1, located in Santa Anna, California.

The conference came about shortly after the first Persian Gulf conflict. At the time of the first Persian Gulf War, the 6252ndGeneral Hospital (USAH), Section 1 in Santa Anna, California was called to active duty. Instead of the hospital being called up in total, the medical staff was called up individually over a several-week period. They were deployed at various locations throughout the world. Once they were deployed, even though the war ended only weeks after people were shipped out, they had to remain on active duty for a one-year period.

Upon initial deployment, it was obvious to me that many people were not ready to be leaving their civilian occupations and families on short notice. The hospital unit had never been deployed in the past to active-duty on this scale and even though they were thoroughly trained, they did not anticipate being called to duty on such short notice. As the former commanding officer of the hospital section, I had the responsibility to notify the 250 to 300 hospital personnel when they were to be shipped out. I recall vividly, the buses rolling in to the Army Reserve Center and calling out people's names that had to board the buses and leave for active-duty. This procedure occurred several times, since people were being deployed individually. As stated in an earlier chapter, it is not good for morale when you train as a unit and get deployed as individuals, not knowing the people you will be working with on active duty.

Since the overall command had a combat stress company, we utilized their staff extensively in setting up the conference and working on the HARRT program. The initial conference was on a Saturday and Sunday in the basement conference room at Camp Pendleton Hospital. The agenda covered many areas and had several speakers. We had a hands-on exercise that involved a terrorist attack taking hostages and these hostages being rescued after being stressed out and then debriefed by the combat stress team.

This was almost the first and last conference, since we had a close call when we did the hostage scenario. Prior to the conference, I met with the security staff at the hospital and explained to them that there would be some strange-looking people coming in the back door of the hospital carrying weapons. I explained it was a training exercise that would be well supervised and the military personnel playing the role of terrorists were Green Beret Special Forces. The Green Berets were instructed specifically to check their weapons in a locked, secured box to be inspected by the guard at the main gate. Approximately a half hour before the exercise was to begin, the Green Berets drove up to the back door of the hospital. When I asked if everything went well at the main gate, they said they did not check in as instructed. I had them get back in their vehicles and return to the main gate and check in. After they did this, we asked people if they would want to experience being taken hostage, and the people who did not were moved to the rear of the classroom as observers.

When the exercise started, the terrorists came in and started the training exercise. The exercise was a tremendous success in demonstrating the effectiveness of the de-briefing of individuals who were highly stressed. There was one situation that we did not expect—one of the observers became so stressed from observing the exercise that she had to be taken aside and individually worked with to calm her down.

Although the first year's conference was a tremendous success, funding for the next four years was nonexistent from the Army organization that allowed me to initiate the conference. In order to continue the conference, I had to call on my family members and friends to help with registration, etc. I did have the availability of some of the staff but no funding for supplies, meals, transportation, and other incidental expenses. During the first five years, approximately 300 to 500 people attended the conference each year. The U.S. Navy and Marines provided most of the support for the conference. The fifth year conference was a milestone. We held this conference at the Army Reserve Center on base and bused approximately 500 people to combat town on base. We had an extensive exercise where soldiers were taken captive and rescued under fire. The combat stress company moved in with their equipment, such as combat stress chambers (large biofeedback units), and did extensive debriefings. All of the major television networks, including ABC, NBC, and CBS, were there reporting on the conference. The conference was not only attended by military personnel, but by the FBI, Los Angeles SWAT, and other police agencies.

At the end of the conference, the Army regional commanding general commented that we, meaning the U.S. Army, had performed a great training exercise. When I asked the general if I could talk to him honestly, he agreed. I explained that except for a few of my immediate staff, the success of the program was largely due to the U.S. Navy and Marines, since they provided all of the personnel, such as the rescuers, as well as the terrorists and the weapons, blank cartridges, and smoke. I explained that the Army provided primarily Meals Ready to Eat (MREs), which had contaminated chocolates removed, and the bus drivers, who drove U.S. Navy buses and got lost on the way to the combat town range. After hearing this, the general instructed me to submit paperwork for any and all funding for the following year. This was the first year that my military organization truly recognized the value of this conference. The conference proceeded for several more years with funding, each conference focusing on various topics. The conference became so successful that there were requests to do an East Coast as well as West Coast conference each year. We had the conference at the Ft. Bragg Kennedy Center (Special Forces Facility) for two years but the distance was too difficult to maintain for my unit and we had to discontinue the conference on the east coast.

The conference actually enabled changes to be made in the military and government. The year we had our focus on prisoners of war, the position paper that we wrote (as we did after every conference) was personally taken to the Veterans Administration and new policies were implemented to assist prisoners of war. We also were able to get Major League Baseball's San Diego Padres to issue lifetime passes to all POWs from WWII and Korea since Vietnam and post-Vietnam POWs had received these passes. Since our prisoner of war conference was so successful in California, we were asked to put on the same conference at the newly built Prisoner of War Museum in Andersonville, Georgia. So many people attended the conference it had to be held in a very large tent adjacent to the museum building.

For the first fifteen years the conference was held at Camp Pendleton; for the next five years it was held in the Los Angeles area; most recently, the conference was located in Carlsbad, California, at the Tri-City Wellness Center. Over the twenty-two years of presentations, I realized the most effective treatment of choice involved treating individuals for combat stress and preparation them for deployment was recognized by many as integrative treatment/wellness programs. The conference was responsible for many constructive programs created to teach individuals how to best work with our veterans. Some of the conference's notable accomplishments were: the Pentagon recommending the utilization of the HARRT program military-wide and making it a part of the combat stress DoD directive, the 2010 congressional hearings looking at the relationship between the use of psychiatric medication and suicide in the military, POW programs being expanded upon by the VA, the development of special POW license plates in California (through the work of Dr. Fernando Tellez, former WWII bomber pilot and POW), the training of thousands of military and civilian personnel on combat stress treatment, increased national recognition of the cause of Combat Stress Reactions (there was an interview by on a national TV network of a combat stress officer in Iraq stating that he was trained at our conference), and the Marine Corps Chemical Biological Radiation team and Army combat stress teams training together for the first time.

During the 21st International Military and Civilian Combat Stress Conference, it became disturbingly apparent to me that years of educating mental health professionals, government officials, and military officials might not improve mental health services to our veterans as rapidly as successful litigation against various government organizations for not providing adequate mental health services.

After several years of operating the Tri-Service Combat Stress Conference, we noticed some people requesting to present and attend from were outside of the United States. We had representatives from military organizations throughout North America, Europe, and Asia attend the conference and present on how their militaries were dealing with combat stress. Since the conference took on an international presence, we decided to change the name to the International Military and Civilian Combat Stress Conference. As the conference evolved, the different methods of dealing with residual effects of combat stress were hotly debated. The conference has always been noted for being very professional and presenting all sides of the issues discussed.

In this vein, when we volunteered to continue the conference after I retired, we assured everyone that the format of the conference would not change and that various treatment modalities would be presented in order to look at all sides of the issues. We felt very strongly that we would not take money from any organization to continue the conference and that the conference would only run as long as people would attend and pay minimal registration fees. I explained at this year's twenty-second annual conference that the fees of the registrants are all that would be necessary to continue the conference each year.

This decision to not accept funding with strings attached has proven to be a correct decision, as we continue to host presenters who share both sides of the issues.

Finally, this conference only addresses the integrative approaches that are proven effective based on prior research, the presenter's experience from his/her field, and post-conference evaluations from individuals attending the conference. There are absolutely no private or governmental organizations influencing topics for any presentation. Rather, presentations are always based on demonstrated success with our veterans in various treatment settings.

CHAPTER 11

VETERAN LAWSUITS AGAINST GOVERNMENT FACILITIES AND VIOLATION OF THE STANDARDS OF CARE FOR THE PSYCHOLOGICAL NEEDS OF OUR VETERANS

The purpose of this chapter is to demonstrate how veterans can be empowered to insist that they receive the best possible mental health treatment for residual effects of combat stress or any other problems resultant from their military experience. Whether this treatment is provided at the VA or from the private sector, it needs to be provided. In a sense, this chapter is a call to action for all veterans, to insist they be provided the best treatment possible for any and all mental health issues that they experience during and/or after their military service.

The veteran should accept no excuses from the VA for time delays in providing treatment that is reasonable and not just a brain-altering pharmaceutical. They should insist on legitimate integrative mental health treatment to help them get back to normal functioning in the community. Appointments should be given immediately if any veteran asks for mental health services.

If the VA does not provide adequate treatment, then one action the veteran can take is to call their congressman immediately. If no results are seen by this action, the next call should be to an attorney. The first situation I describe in this chapter is an example of a Marine that took legal action and was successful. In a sense, this Marine fired a warning shot across the bow of the VA's mental health programs, telling them they were not doing their job.

Every veteran must step up and assume leadership in getting the quality medical services they were promised; every veteran who is not provided the care he/she is entitled to must step up and assume a leadership role in getting people at the VA to do their jobs. If the VA drags their feet, we must seek viable alternatives from community integrative mental health treatment programs and continue to push the VA to pay for this treatment. In other words, if the government can't do the job, step aside. It's time to demonstrate what was said in the movie *Network*, "I'm mad as hell and not going to take it anymore."

SUCCESSFUL LITIGATION AGAINST THE VA FOR POOR MENTAL HEALTH SERVICES IN PENNSYLVANIA

During September of 2012 I was visiting my family in northeastern Pennsylvania where there was a major trial taking place in the federal courthouse in the town of Scranton, Pennsylvania. Since my brother-in-law is an attorney he was aware of the proceedings, which involved a Marine veteran filing suit against the Veterans Administration. Coincidently, my sister knew the attorneys who were representing the Marine since they were long-time family acquaintances.

Stanley Loskowski III and his wife, Marisol, know what happens when an overburdened VA hospital fails a veteran. The following reprint tells their story better than I could. This reprint of the January 17, 2013 article "Carbondale Veteran Wins 3.7M in Suit Against VA," written by staff writer Steve McConnell, is generously given for this book by the Times-Tribune of Scranton, Pennsylvania.

Carbondale veteran wins $3.7M in suit against VA
STEVE McConnell
Publication Date: January 17, 2013 Page: 1 Section: A Edition: FINAL

A federal judge on Wednesday awarded $3.7 million to an Iraq War veteran from Carbondale who sued the U.S. Department of Veterans' Affairs after his war-induced post-traumatic stress disorder worsened because the agency prescribed him the wrong medication and treated him over the telephone.

Senior U.S. District Judge James M. Munley made the ruling in favor of Stanley Laskowski III, 34, and his wife, Marisol, after a civil nonjury trial before the judge at federal court in Scranton.

"The Laskowskis are very humble and courageous people. They had the courage to serve this country in war and to pursue this case under difficult circumstances," said Scranton attorney Daniel T. Brier, who along with attorney John B. Dempsey represented them in the September trial. "Today, they received justice."

Mr. Laskowski, a decorated Marine sergeant and veteran of Operation Iraqi Freedom, was honorably discharged in February 2007. He has waited just two months shy of three years for a resolution in his case.

In the medical malpractice lawsuit filed in 2010, Mr. Laskowski claimed clinicians at the VA Medical Center in Plains Twp. did not adequately treat his PTSD, prescribed him the wrong medications and did not immediately offer him the best therapeutic methods to alleviate his declining condition.

He testified at the trial of the violence he experienced during the war.

But during his testimony, he couldn't bring himself to talk about the moment he pushed through an apartment door in Baghdad during a sweep of buildings and saw on the floor a dying child, covered in blood.

"I had to get into that door," Mr. Laskowski testified. "I really don't want to get into that, if that's all right."

Earlier in the trial before Mr. Laskowski took the stand, he had to leave the courtroom when Mr. Brier had his expert medical witness describe the bloody scenes in Iraq that fueled the veteran's worsening psychological condition.

Dr. Harvey Dondershine, MD, JD, a Stanford University psychiatrist, said Mr. Laskowski's mental tailspin began when he stormed that apartment building.

When he approached the door and heard the mumbling of human voices within, he shot at the door's lock so he could get inside. When the door cracked open, he saw the child on the floor and believed he was responsible, Dr. Dondershine testified.

Amid other gruesome moments he encountered, Mr. Laskowski came across the remains of a 6-month-old baby amid the shattered debris of an exploded home, Dr. Dondershine testified.

In Judge Munley's 69-page ruling, he agreed with the defense's case that clinicians with the local VA should never have prescribed Mr. Laskowski new medications or changed his medications over the telephone to treat his PTSD.

Also when Mr. Laskowski first sought help in April 2007, he was not treated by a physician for several months and instead dealt mainly with "physician extenders" — medical professionals like nurses and physician's assistants, the judge wrote.

In addition, clinicians did not immediately offer psychotherapy to help him overcome nightmares, paranoia, insomnia and flashbacks spawned by his gruesome wartime experiences, according to court testimony.

The lack of appropriate care worsened his condition, causing him to make the rash choice to break into a pharmacy in Olyphant and steal prescription medications, his attorneys argued.

Judge Munley said his ruling should not be interpreted as a sweeping indictment of the VA.

"We emphasize again, that this case is very fact-specific and our holding applies only to" Mr. Laskowski, Judge Munley said in his ruling. "Our decision should not be interpreted as a sweeping criticism of the care that the (VA) provides to the nation's veterans."

The government's attorney, G. Michael Thiel, contended clinicians did prescribe him the correct medications and that Mr. Laskowski failed to disclose the entirety of his worsening condition to them.

They also scheduled appointments for him to come in and be treated, but he canceled the appointments, according to court testimony.

"He went to Iraq to fight the enemy," Mr. Brier said. "He never expected to come home and fight his own government. We need to protect our protectors. The VA should pay this verdict without further delay in recognition of Sgt. Laskowski's sacrifice to this country."

The VA has paid out approximately $100 Million a year lately to settle malpractice claims to about 3,000 veterans.[114]

The current difficulty with veterans filing litigation against the government, pharmaceutical companies, and psychiatrists is the extensive cost of retaining attorneys. Numerous veterans and their family members who have been damaged by inappropriate mental health treatment all echo the fact that they cannot afford attorneys, but with continuing success, this will also change.

THE EDDIE RAY ROUTH TRIAL FOR THE KILLING OF CHRIS KYLE

On February 24, 2015, Eddie Ray Routh was convicted of murdering Chris Kyle (the famed "American Sniper") on the shooting range where Chris Kyle brought veterans for what he considered therapy—shooting targets.

The defense was trying to prove mental illness, but there should have been testimony focusing on the significant difference between someone being mentally ill and someone demonstrating behavior that is consistent with brain-altering psychiatric medication and illegal drugs.

Routh was convicted. Perhaps he should have been. However, the connection between Routh's actions on that day and the cocktail of prescription and illegal drugs in his system should not be ignored. "The Attorneys Guide To Defending Veterans in

---

114 (https://www.lawyersandsettlements.com/lawsuit/veteran_medical_malpractice.html#. VlSPNoRRy-J)

Criminal Court," by Brockton D. Hunter, Esq., and Ryan C. Else, Esq. has an entire chapter devoted to "The Over-Prescription of Psychotropic Drugs for Military Personnel." In my research, many of the mass shootings that have made the news in recent years have a connection with the prescription of brain-altering drugs.

On December 20, 2013, Journalist Laura Beil wrote a story about the Routh family. It was published in Men's Health magazine and was titled, "Who Killed Chris Kyle?"[115] The story indicated that Chris Kyle's killer, Eddie Routh, was taken to the Dallas Veterans' Affairs Medical Center multiple times by his family prior to the shooting. Although he was diagnosed on July 23, 2011 with PTSD, no significant treatment results appeared showing significant improvement, although there were about 500 pages of medical records written.

The records indicate Eddie Routh may have been offered up to eight different brain-altering psychiatric medications. There was indication of group therapy, but he rarely had individual therapy. His mother stated that her son showed no benefits from the group therapy. His mother also indicated that her son had cognitive problems so severe that in January 2013, she had to answer questions for him when she brought him to the VA.

As previously discussed, in Dr. Peter Breggin's (MD) book, *Medication Madness*, a patient who took psychiatric medications for a short period of time began to contemplate suicide and homicide. In his search for a firearm, he ran down a police

---

115 http://www.menshealth.com/best-life/who-killed-chris-kyle.

officer with his car and tried to obtain the officer's sidearm. This adverse reaction to a psychiatric medication eventually caused all charges to be dropped. How many of the recent mass killings, suicides, and homicides are directly linked to such an adverse reaction? We'll never know.

CHAPTER 12

CORRELATION BETWEEN MASS SHOOTINGS AND PSYCHIATRIC MEDICATIONS

Just as this book was going into the final editing stage, there were two additional mass murders in the United States.

On July 16, 2015, in Chattanooga, Tennessee, Muhammad Youssef Abdulazeez was responsible for a drive-by shooting at a military recruiting center; his second target was a Navy reserve center. Four Marines were killed instantly, a Navy sailor was mortally wounded and died two days later, and a police officer was also wounded. Abdulazeez was killed by police.

When I initially heard of this shooting, it appeared that the shooter was a terrorist. As the story developed, after days of investigation, the Washington Post revealed that Muhammad

Youssef Abdulazeez was on and off antidepressants and also used other illegal drugs. "In a statement by his family, they indicated Abdulazeez's mental illness had contributed to the crime. They revealed that for many years, their son suffered from depression. They also stated that it grieves them beyond belief to know that their son's pain" found its expression in this heinous act of violence." [116]

The shooter's parents told reporters that they were upset their son had firearms and did not want the guns in the house. It was not clear if they just didn't like guns or if they were concerned that their mentally ill son could misuse them.

On July 23, 2015, three people, including the shooter, were killed in a movie theater in Lafayette, Louisiana. Two died at the scene, including the gunman, and a third person was hospitalized. Authorities said nine other people were wounded. "The gunman, identified as 59-year-old John Russel Houser, fired at least 13 times from a handgun, police said." [117]

Many people see mass shooters who are medicated as capable of logically planning and following through with their actions, but it's important to understand that their actions are based on delusional thinking resulting from brain-altering medications. Their anger and despair is important to recognize, but not as important as the distorted reasoning for their actions.

---

116 https://www.washingtonpost.com/politics/chattanooga-shooter-an-aimless-young-man-who-smoked-dope-and-shot-guns/2015/07/18/c213f6a6-2d7d-11e5-a5ea-cf74396e59ec_story.html
117 http://nypost.com/2015/07/23/theater-shooting-in-louisiana-leaves-at-least-2-dead/

To understand how a person acts when under the influence of brain-altering medications, consider the effect that alcohol has. While under the influence, people will often have terrible judgment. There are instances when people who are intoxicated will become violent or angry, even if they've never done so when sober. Psychiatric medications are more powerful and longer lasting than a one-night binge, which results in longer-term poor judgment and reasoning, which distorts reality.

So why do people become violent when on brain-altering substances? Because when you interfere with the natural chemistry of the brain, you don't really know what the outcome will be. It can range from happiness to anger and can include both poles within a very short period of time. When the higher human functioning parts of the brain are interfered with, the more basic, animalistic parts of the brain become more active. This part of the brain does not possess reasoning and judgment capabilities; it just acts to help the person survive the real or imagined dangers.

We need to realize that primitive and uncivilized people most intensely meet their needs for survival and power (self-worth, achievement) by taking someone's life. Civilized people, with intact higher-level brain functioning, meet this need for power by speaking to people and offering advice. You see this on a daily basis from parents, schoolteachers, politicians, and entertainers. Whether the audience is a few people or thousands, the feeling of power is met.

CHAPTER 13

ADDITIONAL
RESOURCES AND
ARTICLES

Below are articles that elaborate more on some of what I have stated in this book. With so much information out there, one has to wonder why nothing has been done to correct these dangers.

David Kupelian is an award-winning journalist, managing editor of WND, editor of Whistleblower magazine, and author of the best-selling book, *The Marketing of Evil*. His newest book, *How Evil Works*, was released to critical acclaim in the spring of 2010. Read more at http://mobile.wnd.com/2013/01/the-giant-gaping-hole-in-sandy-hook-reporting/#qRZDsWg7sZLxtPKk.99

Carey, B. (2011, August 2). Drugs Found Ineffective for Veterans' Stress. New York Times. Retrieved from http://www.nytimes.com/2011/08/03/health/research/03psych.html

Bernardy, Nancy (2013, September 28). The Role of Benzodiaz-epines in the Treatment of Posttraumatic Stress Disorder (PTSD). PTSD Research Quarterly 23.04:1-3. Retrieved 23 Nov. 2015, from http://www.ptsd.va.gov/professional/newsletters/research-quarterly/v23n4.pdf

Chedekel, L. (2013, February 21). Within Connecticut, New Ha-ven area has highest use of antidepressants, study finds." New Have Register News. Retrieved from http://www.nhregister.com/article/NH/20130221/NEWS/302219985

Dao, James. (2013, February 6). Study Seeks Biomarkers for In-visible War Scars. The New York Times. Retrieved Novem-ber 23, 2015 from http://www.nytimes.com/2013/02/07/us/study-seeks-biomarkers-for-ptsd-and-traumatic-brain-injuries.html.

Glantz, A. (2010, October 16). After Service, Veteran Deaths Surge. New York Times. Retrieved from http://www.ny-times.com/2010/10/17/us/17bcvets.html?_r=0

Harris, G. (2011, March 17). New Efficiencies taking toll on psychiatry talk therapy no longer pays. New York Times. Retrieved November 13, 2015, from http://www.nytimes.com/2011/03/06/health/policy/06doctors.html?pagewant-ed=all

Kime, P. (2012, May 3). Pentagon to limit antipsychotic drugs for PTSD. The Marine Corps Time. Retrieved from http://archive.Marinecorpstimes.com/article/20120503/

NEWS/205030316/Pentagon-limit-antipsychot-ic-drugs-PTSD

Miller, K. (2012, July 25). Military Faces Suicide "Epidemic" Panetta Tells Congress. Retrieved from http://www.bloomberg.com/news/articles/2012-07-25/military-faces-suicide-epidemic-panetta-tells-u-s-lawmakers

Murphy, K. (2012, April 12). A fog of drugs and war. Los Angeles Time. Retrieved from http://articles.latimes.com/2012/apr/07/nation/la-na-Army-medication-20120408

O'Meara, K.P., (2013, September 18). Navy Yard shooter was on Antidepressant Trazodone—How many more drug induced shootings until lawmakers wake up? Retrieved from http://www.cchrint.org/2013/09/18/navy-yard-shooter-was-on-antidepressant-trazodone/

Robinson, J. (2008, May 24). Vets taking PTSD drugs die in sleep – Hurricane man's death the 4th in West Virginia. Charleston Gazette. Retrieved from https://tmap.wordpress.com/2008/05/24/vets-taking-ptsd-drugs-die-in-sleep-hurricane-mans-death-the-4th-in-west-virginia/

Sell, D. (2012, May 14). Military taking steps to limit use of antipsychotics for PTSD. Philly.com. Retrieved from http://articles.philly.com/2012-05-14/business/31690187_1_seroquel-andrew-ptsd

Tighman, A. (2010, May 26). Psychiatric Drugs Killing U.S. Military Vets In Their Sleep. Marine Corps Times.

Thompson, M. (2008, June 5). America's Medicated Army. Retrieved November 13, 2015, from http://content.time.com/time/magazine/article/0,9171,1812055,00.html

Williams, T. (2012, June 8). Suicides outpacing war deaths for troops. New York Times. Retrieved from http://www.nytimes.com/2012/06/09/us/suicides-eclipse-war-deaths-for-us-troops.html

Five days before this book was to be released, an article was written in the San Diego Union Tribune that again illustrates what this book has been describing. Steele, J. (2016, January 10). Report Says VA Failed In Care Of Veteran. San Diego Union Tribune.[118]

The article discusses the suicide of a thirty-five-year old Camp Pendleton Marine, Jeremy Sears, at an Oceanside gun range in October 2014; I want to elaborate on this tragedy.

For me, this story hits close to home since I personally know many Marines at Camp Pendleton and have even used the Oceanside indoor gun range on numerous occasions. Ever since this tragic death, there have been organizations and people that I know well, such as the American Combat Veterans Of War (ACVOW) and retired Marine General Attorney David Brahms, questioning the VA's treatment of Sgt. Sears.

As a result of their questioning, the VA's own inspector general finally investigated the claim that Sgt. Sears fell through

---

118   Retrieved from http://www.sandiegouniontribune.com/news/2016/jan/10/va-report-jeremy-sears-veteran-suicide/#sthash.am7r0ZFo.dpuf

the cracks in their system. This investigation revealed a measure of confirmation that the VA mishandled Sgt. Sears' treatment. The newspaper article states that the "report reveals that San Diego VA doctors continued to prescribe a narcotic painkiller— hydrocodone drug known as Vicodin—for 22 months without any oversight, even though studies have warned that chronic pain elevates the risk of suicide attempts. And, high suicide risk makes use of hydrocodone less appropriate."

As I have mentioned previously in this book, research has shown that there is a link between TBI and suicide. Also, the adverse reactions of narcotic medication and psychiatric medications have a black box warning; the first adverse event is identified as suicide. The newspaper article states that "overall, the VA inspector general's analysis said the San Diego VA erred in several ways during the nearly two years Sears was under its care."

I believe that one of the only ways that people can be identified and held responsible for this travesty is through formal litigation similar to what occurred in the Pennsylvania VA case mentioned in Chapter One.

LIST OF ANTIDEPRESSANT DRUGS WITH MEDICATION GUIDES

Anafranil (clomipramine)

Asendin (amoxapine)

Aventyl (nortriptyline)

Celexa (citalopram hydrobromide)

Cymbalta (duloxetine)

Desyrel (trazodone HCl)

Elavil (amitriptyline)

Effexor (venlafaxine HCl)

Emsam (selegiline)

Etrafon(perphenazine/amitriptyline)

fluvoxamine maleate Lexapro (escitalopram oxalate)

Limbitrol (chlordiazepoxide/amitriptyline)

Ludiomil (maprotiline)

Marplan (isocarboxazid)

Nardil (phenelzine sulfate)

nefazodone HCl Norpramin (desipramine HCl)

Pamelor (nortriptyline)

Parnate (tranylcypromine sulfate)

Paxil (paroxetine HCl)

Pexeva (paroxetine mesylate)

Prozac (fluoxetine HCl)

Remeron (mirtazapine)

Sarafem (fluoxetine HCl)

Seroquel (quetiapine)

Sinequan (doxepin)

Surmontil (trimipramine)

Symbyax (olanzapine/fluoxetine)

Tofranil (imipramine)

Tofranil-PM (imipramine pamoate)

Triavil (perphenazine/amitriptyline)

Vivactil (protriptyline)

Wellbutrin (bupropion HCl)

Zoloft (sertraline HCl)

Zyban (bupropion HCl).

In addition to all the articles I reference in this book, I would like to recognize the brand new song that Macklemore and Ryan Lewis performed at the American Music Awards Sunday night (11-23-15). Soul singer Leon Bridges lent his talents to the song, titled "Kevin."

The lyrics tell the tragic story of not only illegal drug substance abuse, but also the story of prescription psychiatric medication abuse. If you connect with what I have been saying in this book, then listening to the song and reading the words is a must.[119]

This performance and message in "Kevin" is, in my eyes, very consistent with the message provided to audiences in the Pulitzer Prize winning play "Next To Normal" [120]

---

119   (https://youtu.be/k-sFbu4K-Zs).
120   http://www.playbill.com/news/article/next-to-normal-wins-2010-pulitzer-prize-for-dra-ma-167584()

ACKNOWLEDGEMENTS

Billings (changed in 1903 from Bellini) and Gillette Family:

Being raised in a large extended family in a Pennsylvania Borough called Dunmore was inspirational throughout my life. Being the oldest of five children with hard-working parents, Mary and Bart (a coal miner and steel worker), provided a strong foundation. This large, loving, and caring family with many aunts, uncles, and cousins provided a lasting sense of love, care, morals, values, and responsibility to this day.

Thank you to the Jesuit College at The University of Scranton for teaching me discipline, responsibility, commitment, and the philosophy of never giving up on your goals. When going through basic training as a combat engineer in the Army, I would joke with my peers that the drill instructors were no match when compared to the Jesuits.

I will always appreciate working with and receiving help from all my subordinates, colleagues, and superior officers in the U.S. Army who helped me realize my dream to create an international combat stress conference that would train our soldiers and their families on how to best deal with the many circumstances of being in the military. Without their support and equal dedication, this book and all it sets out to accomplish could never have been started.

Thank you to all the combat stress conference presenters over the twenty-two years since the international combat stress conference has been occurring. Without their expertise and presentations, the conference that spurred this book would not have been possible. They led me to strongly believe, over the evolution of the conference, that integrative treatment is the treatment of choice for any and all residual effects of combat stress.

ABOUT THE AUTHOR

DR. BART P BILLINGS has been working in the fields of mental health, human services, and program development/management for over forty-eight years. He possesses licenses in clinical psychology and marriage and family therapy, was a certified rehabilitation counselor, a credential as a community college counselor, and was an Elkins Award recipient as Counselor of the Year for California. In February of 2014, he received the International Human Rights Award from the Citizens Commission on Human Rights International (CCHR).

Dr. Billings has an extensive background in management and program development, which includes, but is not limited to, chief of professional services/assistant director at the UC Davis Medical Center's Department of Physical Medicine & Rehabilitation. He also founded the Institute for Occupational Services (IOS) in Sacramento, California. He was the commanding officer (CO) for a U.S. Army Reserve general hospital section and has served a total of approximately thirty-four years in the U.S. Army as an enlisted soldier and as an officer. His highest military rank was colonel (SCNG-SC as medical directorate). He founded and directed: The Annual International Military and Civilian Combat

Stress Conferences (initially called the Tri-Service Combat Stress Conference at Camp Pendleton California), Prisoner of War Conferences, and the military-wide Human Assistance Rapid Response Team (HARRT), which was accepted at the Pentagon in 1997 as a military readiness protocol.

He was recently a guest on HBO's Vice News, and has previously been on ABC's Nightline and U.S. News and World Report. He has also been featured on various national and international documentaries, TV news shows, and extensive radio shows to discuss combat stress. He has given testimony at congressional and state legislative hearings on the need for better mental health treatment programs for military personnel and their families. Some of these hearings resulted in the awarding of multi-million dollar Department Of Defense grants for national research on how to improve treatment for post-traumatic stress disorder and traumatic brain injuries. He is responsible for initiating congressional hearings held on February 24, 2010 and providing congressional hearing testimony on the relationship between psychiatric medication and increased suicides in the military (available on the Congressional Record). In September 2012, he lectured to some of the psychology and leadership faculty at the U.S. Army's Military Academy at West Point. On June 5, 2003, he was named a member of the Governor's Advisory Board to Patton State Hospital, California. He has worked overseeing all psychological services for the San Diego district of the California Department of Rehabilitation. He has developed residential treatment programs in substance abuse and alcoholism, as well as human assistance programs for the civilian and military community.

Recently he wrote a chapter in the book *Attorneys Guide to Defending Veterans in Criminal Court*. He is a member of the National Center for Youth Law Medical and Scientific Advisory Board. Dr. Billings was a senior faculty at the William Glasser, MD Institute for over thirty years and has taught classes at the University of San Francisco, University of California Davis, and United States International University, as well as workshops on counseling and management throughout the United States. He speaks on health and nutrition with a focus on the psychology of eating. As prior owner and operator of a restaurant for four years, he practiced his teachings.

He was the founder and president of a manufacturing company called TBH Productions that produced OmniSonic professional audio loudspeakers. His work with sound and his vast experience in the medical field has resulted in him writing an article in Navy Medicine titled, "The Sound You Feel Can Be Dangerous To Your Health" (Jan-Feb 2002, p.22-26), which deals with Vibroacoustic disease.

He was awarded an Honorary Chaplain Certificate from the Georgia State Defense Force. He has also volunteered for charities as a performing arts/special events director, producer, and writer for over thirty years. He has directed The All American Festival, which raised funds for veterans' scholarships. He was also one of the producers for "Proud To Be An American Day," which drew 150,000 people in Oceanside, California.

From April 2010 until November 17, 2012, he owned a popular restaurant/bar in La Costa, California, drawing a large number of retired and active duty veterans who often spoke to Dr. Billings about their own personal issues with combat stress.

In 2015, he was asked to be a commissioner for the CCHR International organization.

He has written numerous professional articles and his first book, *Development of a Community Transitional Rehabilitation Program*, focused on vocational and personal growth as it applies to the mentally ill, with a special emphasis on drug addiction and personality disorders. His current book, *Invisible Scars—Treating Combat Stress and PTSD without Medication,* covers over forty years of his work with combat stress residual effects on our veterans and their families.

www.bartpbillings.com

IMPORTANT ISSUES SINCE THE 1ST EDITION

1. A REPORT FROM THE FRONT LINES OF A MARINE CORPS LEAGUE PROGRAM DEALING WITH COMBAT STRESS

One of the uses of this book *Invisible Scars*, is proving to be effective and helpful to our veterans, which is described below by a Marine.

David T. Ossian
Asst. National Vice Commandant
Midwest Division
Marine Corps League

Once A Marine—Always A Marine

A few months ago a friend of mine gave me the good Doctor's book as a gift. It was signed by the author and I was excited. My friend didn't express to me how much this book could change my life.

By the time I got to page 25 I felt compelled to speak to Dr. Billings and asked my friend how he got me this book. He explained his relationship with Doc's son in law and offered to put us in touch. 30 minutes later and my phone rings. Since that day I have been on a mission.

I created a Facebook event and hosted a Book Club—Peer Support Group at my home. 16 Marines and FMF Corpsman showed up the first night. Several more studied on their own with email-text-Facebook feedback to me. We started by watching Dr. Billings video on his website (www.bartpbillings.com). We then discussed expectations and challenges. Before anyone left we all agreed that everyone would take at least one other person's cell phone number for contact in case the book brought out a difficult demon.

On the night of the second meeting we watched the first half of a documentary that Dr Billings was in called, "Hidden Enemy" (http://www.cchr.org/documentaries/the-hidden-enemy.html) and then discussed our thoughts on Chapter 1. I did my best to facilitate the conversation and make sure that everyone contributed. The comments and conversations were extremely impactful and healthy. We planned to read and discuss one chapter every two weeks.

During our third meeting my co-facilitator Retired USN Senior Chief Petty Officer and FMF Corpsman guided us through setting our own rules. He then produced a 3 foot clipboard and wrote them out in sharpy as the team responded with ideas:

- No interrupting.
- No derogatory statements
- Stay on the subject matter

These are just a few examples. There are several other great ones that I will have to write them all down and share.

After we discussed ground rules we discussed Chapter 2 and watched two TED talks. Both were short videos about Veteran's issues.

Jake Wood's and Sebastian Junger's. Both are amazing talks.

At our next meeting we are having a guest who is an internal medicine Doctor (non VA) to discuss with the team what these drugs really do to the body. This will be anonymously.

We will be ordering 100 more books this week to get two more of our Nebraska teams studying and then I will encourage our women's Auxiliary to start a book study as well to better understand their husbands and sons.

To summarize: I am a Desert Storm Veteran who needed purpose in my life. I joined the Marine Corps League 6 years ago and have been extremely successful, but this will top everything I have done to date as far as helping Veterans. Properly marketed and delivered this model could have serious impact on mental health and the overall quality of life for our Veterans. I am meeting tonight with the regional head of the Wounded Warrior Regiment for the Marine Corps and I am taking him a copy of the book for him to read on his upcoming flight to Camp Pendleton.

I thank you Sir for taking the time to read this and for your input on how I can continue to change Veteran's and their families lives.

God bless and Semper Fidelis
David T. Ossian
Asst. National Vice Commandant
Midwest Division
Marine Corps League
Nebraskamcl@gmail.com
www.midwestdivisionmarinecorpsleague.org
Cell: 402-580-3489

A follow up email reads:

Sir,

I am very proud to be fighting this battle with you.

Last night we had an amazing book club – Peer group meeting. It would be difficult to put into words the impact and intensity of this extremely positive meeting. We were discussing Chapter 4 and many of the Marines and Corpsman spoke of how this chapter scared the hell out of them. The idea of taking the medication prescribed by a Doctor and dying in you sleep is tough to process. During our 2 hour discussion we spoke in depth about how difficult it is to deal with guilt. The only mental health issue not addressed in the DSM. Guilt might be the universal connection that we all share and of course disappointment. The reality of the potential impact of what we are doing is not lost on my team. They see the big picture and the grass roots movement that we are part of.

Our Omaha team will be starting a separate Peer Group – book club in their area next week.

God willing we can build an ideal model of a life altering Veteran's Service Organization.

---

2. YOU MAY WANT TO ASK PEOPLE TO CALL OR WRITE THEIR SENATOR AND CONGRESSMAN TO SUPPORT THE FOLLOWING.

The current Senate Bill by John Mc Cain – S.788 – 115th Congress (2017-2018)/VeteranOvermedication Prevention Act of 2017. Also presented by the House Of Representatives is a companion bill; H.R.2652 – Veteran Overmedication Prevention Act of 2017, Sponsored by Rep. Mike Coffman [R-CO-6] introduced 05/25/17.

Hopefully these bills will provide more integrative treatment for our military Vets, without the use of brain altering, non-effective, destructive psychiatric medications. Also it is imperative that more physiatrists be hired by the VA to work with our vets. A physiatrist is a Physical Medicine & Rehabilitation (PM&R) medical doctor who specializes in treating physical and mental difficulties. This specialty can be seen as one "Born of War," going back to after WW I, when PM&R was the treatment of choice for our war veterans.

Although the government states that there are 20 veteran suicides a day (Figure released by the government in 2016) in the US, this figure is an underestimate, since several states don't report specific veteran suicides. This suicide rate has been reported in the past several years as 22 suicides a day, which was still an underestimation.

Related to this high suicide rate is the fact that in 2010, the number of veterans filling a prescription for brain altering psychiatric medications (All have black box warnings of suicidality as the first adverse effect) was 1.85 million veterans filling at least one prescription. From 2005 thru 2011, the Department of Defense increased the amount of psychiatric medications purchased by about 700%. From 2001 through 2011, the VA spent $1.64 billion just on benzodiazepines and the antipsychotics Risperdal and Seroquel.

PTSD has been a label placed on 37% of recent war veterans with 80% of those being given brain altering psychiatric medications.of these vets, 89% were prescribed antidepressants and 34% were prescribed antipsychotics. The psychiatric community has failed to realize that PTS (Without "D") is a normal reaction for most people that have been in combat. It's a shame that government spent $3 billion on "PTSD treatments" for veterans in 2012 alone, without realizing that PTS is a normal reaction to being in an abnormal environment. With the proper amount of time and supportive integrative treatment, this normal reactions, associated with the abnormal experience of combat, i.e., hyper vigilance, nightmares,… etc., can be reversed with much less monies being spent.

One must remember that in WW II , veterans were identified with Battle Fatigue, not a label of Battle Fatigue Disorder. This is because the medical community realized that Battle Fatigue was a normal reaction to being in combat. Veterans simply got fatigued from fighting and with proper rest and relaxation (R&R), most returned to normal functioning. This is not occurring today, since psychiatry is in the business of medicating most of their patients with brain altering drugs that don't work and in some situations, Electro Convulsive Therapy (ETC) that also destroys healthy brain cells.

The lack of proper treatment of our vets has resulted in the VA's mental health budget increasing from about $3 billion in 2003 to $7.5 billion in 2016. If any military person had a higher than average number of deaths for the troops they were responsible for, they would be relieved and possibly court-martialed. If a corporate officer, in the civilian community, were responsible for significant financial losses, they would be fired and replaced. So one can ask the question, why the people responsible for veterans mental health (Psychiatry in general as a profession), and the consistent loss of lives to suicide , haven't been fired and replaced? This is a question that must be answered!

REFERENCES

Invisible Scars, by Bart P Billings,Ph.D, Feb 2016
www.bartpbillings.com
http://www.militarytimes.com/story/veterans/2016/07/07/Va-suicide-20-daily-research/86788332/.
Ilse R. Wiechers, MD, MPP, et al., "Increased Risk Among Older Veterans of Prescribing Psychotropic Medication in the Absence of Psychiatric Diagnoses," Am J. Geriatr Psychiatry, Jun 2014.
"VA/Defense Mental Health Drug Expenditures Since 2001," May 2012 Drug Totals, Government Executive, http://cdn.govex-ec.com/media/gbc/docs/pdfs_edit/051712bb1_may2012drugto-tals.pdf.

Susan Donaldson James, "Marines Battalion Mentally Upbeat, Despite Record Deaths," ABC News, April 15, 2011, http://www.abcnews.go.com/Health/camp-pendleton-marine-battalion-mentally-fit-deadliest-war/story?id=13377215; Mohamed S, Rosenheck RA, "Pharmacotherapy of PTSD in the US Department of Veterans Affairs: diagnostic- and symptom-guided drug selection," Journal of Clinical Psychiatry, 2008, June Vol. 69, No. 6, pp. 959-65, http://www.ncbi.nlm.nih.gov/pubmed/18588361.

Mohamed S., et al., "Pharmacotherapy of PTSD in the U.S. Department of Veterans Affairs: diagnostic- and symptom-guided drug selection," J. Clin Psychiatry, Jun 2008, https://www.ncbi.nlm.nih.gov/pubmed/18588361.

John Ramsey, "The Last Battle: Steven Chadduck lost his home and nearly committed suicide while waiting for help for PTSD," Fayottesville Observer, Sept. 24, 2012, fayobserver.com/military/article_a0699933-cac5-5ced-8616-f01eef305f16.html; Leo Shane III, "Budget deal nails down fiscal 2016 spending for DoD, VA," Military Times, 16 Dec 2015, http://www.militarytimes.com/story/military/2015/12/16/budget-omnibus-fy16-defense-veterans-affairs-pentagon/77416466/.

Alan Zarembo, "Government's PTSD treatment for veterans lacking, report finds," Los Angeles Times, 20 Jun 2014, http://www.latimes.com/nation/la-na-ptsd-report-20140621-story.html.

Alan Zarembo, "Government's PTSD treatment for veterans lacking, report finds," Los Angeles Times, 20 Jun 2014, http://www.latimes.com/nation/la-na-ptsd-report-20140621-story.html.

"Let's Stop Using Experimental Vaccines and Psych Drugs that are Destroying our Veterans and Military Personnel," Health Impact News, 2014, http://healthimpactnews.com/2014/lets-stop-using-experimental-vaccines-and-psych-drugs-that-are-destroying-our-veterans-and-military-personnel/.
Bart P. Billings,Ph.D.

---

3. JUST WONDERING WHY STILL 22 SUICIDES A DAY (GOV'T NOW STATES 20 WHICH IS UNDERESTIMATE) FOR VETS.

With all the statistics being thrown around during the most recent election year (2016), i.e., number of murders in inner cities, victims of illegal aliens, etc., the figure of 22 veterans committing suicide each day (approx. 8,030 a year) gets lost in the shuffle for Vets.

Gov't in 2016 states 20 vet suicides a day, which is an underestimate, since not all places count veterans suicides, especially vets on VA waiting list for mental health services that never get seen. This suicide rate has been going on for many years and little seems to be done by the government to help this large number of veterans, who have served our country with distinction.

When I ask myself WHY ??? I start thinking what possible reason could their be for this negligence? Is it purposeful that nothing has been done to help these vets? Who would do such a thing, I wonder? Heaven forbidden that I even allude to a conspiracy — not me!

Here are some of the things that go through my wondering mind:

1. The profession generally in charge of Mental Health Services in the Veterans Administration and Military

is Psychiatry (As well as in the civilian community). As I noted in my book, "Invisible Scars," Psychiatry's primary treatment modality is brain altering psychiatric medication, that have a severe BLACK BOX warning, that lists suicide as the first side effect. Now consider that the field of psychiatry and the big-pharma companies (that produce psychiatric medications) generate 1/3 of a trillion dollars a year dispensing these drugs.

2. Then I think, that if 8,030 vets a year are removed from receiving medical benefits, retirement income, social security, etc., how much money is the government saving on these expenditures each year for many years.

3. How could our country, with so many brilliant scientists, fail to solve the problem of suicide among our veteran population. We are the country that put men on the moon almost 50 years ago. We cured Polio and many other diseases?

4. Is a consistent 22 Veteran suicides a day (Some professional veteran groups think it is more) for such a long period of time coincidental or is it purposeful?

5. Why do we hear the excuse from the governments mental health mouthpiece (psychiatry), that there is no silver bullet to solve the problem. Could it be that they are looking for ONE SILVER BULLET that is a drug. If you are old enough, you will remember that the Lone Ranger had a whole belt of silver bullets to solve law-

lessness in the old west. I call this integrative treatment in mental health?

6. When we are presently loosing now and over the past several years, so many of our battle proven, best patriots to suicide, more than in current combat, more than being murdered in major individual inner cities, more than to criminal illegal aliens, why is this not the main issue in this years election?

Just wondering!!
Bart P. Billings,Ph.D.

---

4. FIVE DAYS BEFORE MY 1ST EDITION BOOK WAS RELEASED, AN ARTICLE WAS WRITTEN IN THE SAN DIEGO UNION TRIBUNE THAT AGAIN ILLUSTRATES WHAT MY BOOK DESCRIBES IN DETAIL.

The article is as follows:

Steele, J. (2016, January 10). Report Says VA Failed In Care Of Veteran. San Diego Union Tribune, Retrieved from http://www.sandiegouniontribune.com/news/2016/jan/10/va-report-jeremy-sears-veteran-suicide/#sthash.am7r0ZFo.dpuf

This is the closing comment in the book in chapter 13 and identifies what I feel is again negligence on the part of the VA, which resulted in the suicide death of a 35 year old Camp Pendleton Marine, Jeremy Sears, at an indoor Oceanside gun range in October 2014; I want to elaborate on this tragedy.

For me, this story hits close to home since I personal know many Marines at Camp Pendleton and have even used the Oceanside indoor gun range on numerous occasions. Ever since this tragic death, their have been organizations and people that I know well, such as the American Combat Veterans Of War (ACVOW) and retired Marine General Attorney David Brahms, questioning the VA's treatment of Sgt. Sears.

As a result of their work, these critics' statements resulted in the VA's own Inspector General finally investigating the claim that Sgt. Sears fell through the cracks in their system. This investigation revealed a measure of confirmation that the VA mishandled Sgt. Sears's treatment. The newspaper article states that the Inspector General's "report reveals that San Diego VA doctors continued to prescribe a narcotic painkiller – hydrocodone drug known as Vicodin – for 22 months without any oversight, even though studies have warned that chronic pain elevates the risk of suicide attempts. And, high suicide risk makes use of hydrocodone less appropriate". Although the newspaper report didn't mention brain altering psychiatric anti-depressant/ anti-psychotic medication being used, I suspect that it was also prescribed.

As I have mentioned previously in my book, research has shown that there is a link between TBI and suicide. Also the adverse reactions of narcotic medication and psychiatric medications have black box warnings, with the first adverse event being identified as suicide. The newspaper article states "Overall, the VA Inspector General's analysis said the San Diego VA erred in several ways during the nearly 2 years Sgt. Sears was under its care".

From my perspective, I feel based on past history that one of the only ways that people can be identified and held responsible for this travesty is through formal litigation, similar to what has occurred in the Pennsylvania VA case that I mention in detail in the book.

---

5. "MY NEW SOLUTION FOR PREVENTING PURCHASES OF FIREARMS BY INDIVIDUALS WITH MENTAL DISORDERS"

With mass shooting in the US, the media and politicians have been stating that something needs to be done in regard to gun control, as well as focusing more on mental health issues and keeping guns out of the hands of individuals that are considered mentally ill.

If the focus on mental health issues requires increasing the numbers of mental health providers, such as psychiatrists, whose primary treatment modality is prescribing brain altering psychiatric medications, then this solution would only increase the problem. It will be adding fuel to the fire. It has been established that most all of the mass shooters were on or previously used prescription brain altering psychiatric medications. Also many of the shooters got their guns legally with background checks. Therefore the issue should be on brain altering psychiatric meds being used.

When increasing the number of mental health providers, we must look at specialties that practice integrative treatment, without the use of psychiatric medications, i.e., psychologists, social workers, counselors, etc.

In my soon to be released book, *INVISIBLE SCARS – How To Treat Combat Stress and PTSD Without Medication*, I discuss and sight research that shows most all mass shooters, over the past decade, have either actively been on or previously been on brain altering psychiatric medications and in some cases, alcohol or illegal drugs as well. Therefore, the focus now should be on "psychiatric medication control" instead of focusing on "gun control".

Since there is such a strong relationship between the mass shootings and brain altering psychiatric medication, it would be common sense to set up a system where anyone taking a brain altering psychiatric medication would not be allowed to purchase or own a firearm.

A reasonable way of accomplishing this would be for: *all pharmacists, filling a prescription for a black box, brain altering psychiatric medication, who normally enter the patient's name into their computer, would at the same time, be linked to the Department of Justice (DOJ) and FBI's data base. Once in the DOJ and FBI system, the person's name would be sent to every firearms retailer in the United States, putting the name on a "cannot buy" a firearm list.*

This way, if the person named on the DOJ "cannot buy" list, comes into a gun store to purchase a weapon, the salesperson would simply say their name is on a "cannot buy" list. The list gives no reason, due to confidentially, and if the person on the list wants to know why they can't purchase a firearm, the salesperson would simply give them the contact information at DOJ, to get an explanation.

I would also recommend that if a relative, with the same last name of the person on the list comes into purchase a firearm, they should be informed that their relative should not have access to the firearm and that they themselves would be liable if this occurs.

Some may say that this may breach confidentiality, but in California and other states, systems are already in place, where if a person has the potential to harm themselves or others, it gets reported before hand to the proper agency.

A good example is when a person is considered to have a lapse of consciousness, due to some type of brain impairment. The physician has a responsibility to report this person to the appropriate source, so the information gets to the Department Of Motor Vehicles.

For example: "California HEALTH AND SAFETY CODE, SECTION 103900 states:

(a) Every physician and surgeon shall report immediately to the local health officer in writing, the name, date of birth, and address of every patient at least 14 years of age or older whom the physician and surgeon has diagnosed as having a case of a disorder characterized by lapses of consciousness. However, if a physician and surgeon reasonably and in good faith believes that the reporting of a patient will serve the public interest, he or she may report a patient's condition even if it may not be required under the department's definition of disorders characterized by lapses of consciousness pursuant to subdivision (d).

(b) The local health officer shall report in writing to the Department of Motor Vehicles the name, age, and address, of every person reported to it as a case of a disorder characterized by lapses of consciousness.

(c) These reports shall be for the information of the Department of Motor Vehicles in enforcing the Vehicle Code, and shall be kept confidential and used solely for the purpose of determining the eligibility of any person to operate a motor vehicle on the highways of this state.

(d) The department, in cooperation with the Department of Motor Vehicles, shall define disorders characterized by lapses of consciousness based upon existing clinical standards for that definition for purposes of this section and shall include Alzheimer's disease and those related disorders that are severe enough to be likely to impair a person's ability to operate a motor vehicle in the definition".

Another system that is already in place, that is even more closely related to potential dangers of prescription brain altering psychiatric medications in California is called, the "Controlled Substance Utilization Review and Evaluation System [CURES) Program".

This program is as follows:

"State of California Department of Justice, Office of the Attorney General

The Department of Justice (DOJ) and the Department of Consumer Affairs (DCA) are pleased to announce that the state's new Controlled Substance Utilization Review and Evaluation System – commonly referred to as "CURES 2.0" – will go live on July 1, 2015. This upgraded prescription drug monitoring program features a variety of performance improvements and added functionality.

The Controlled Substance Utilization Review and Evaluation System (CURES) is a database containing information on Schedule II through IV controlled substances dispensed in California. It is a valuable investigative, preventive, and educational tool for the healthcare community, regulatory boards, and law enforcement".

Therefore, as one can see, mechanisms are already in existence that can be slightly altered to add brain altering psychiatric medications. There are actually some brain altering psychiatric medications (Controlled Substance) on the CURES list that are already identified as Schedule II controlled substances; to mention a few i.e.; Amphetamine – Adderall, Dextroamphetamine (Dexedrine), Lisdexamfetamine (Vyvanse) used for the treatment of ADHD and narcolepsy. Also listed is Methylphenidate (Ritalin, Concerta), Dexmethylphenidate(Focalin), for treatment of ADHD, narcolepsy. Additionally, this applies to Methamphetamine for treatment of ADHD, severe obesity. There are many more brain altering medications prescribed by physicians, being used for mental health patients, on this schedule II list.

As you can see from the above, there are already systems in place that can be added to, that can identify individuals that have a mental disorder, that are on brain altering psychiatric medications. By implementing my suggested above program as prescribed, the number of people with mental disorders, having access to legally purchasing a firearm, would be dramatically reduced.

Also, I feel that the FDA should have the pharmaceutical companies, include in their Medication Guide, which patients and their families are supposed to be given, by the physician prescribing brain altering "Black Box" psychiatric medications, the following information: "Individuals taking this medication should not have access to firearms".

*This information is a portion of copyrighted material from "Invisible Scars" by Bart Billings, PhD.

---

6. EXCERPTS FROM CHAPTER 4 REGARDING MY OPINION CTE

I strongly feel all NFL football players (And many others who play football), to a degree, have experienced CTE. My comment was based on the nature of the sport and the 4-22-15 article in USA Today; "Judge Approves Potential $1 Billion Settlement To Resolve NFL Concussion Lawsuit," which reported that 6000 retired NFL players will receive an average of $190K for concussion injuries. This is a significant number composed of approximately 1/3 of all retired players. This number accounts only for those experiencing problems while the other 2/3 have yet to see problems or they are minimal based on the degree of CTE experienced.(http://www.usatoday.com/story/sports/nfl/2015/04/22/nfl-concussion-lawsuit-settlement-judge-1-billion/26192827/)

Since anyone with a TBI or CTE has an increased risk of suicide four times more than someone without this injury combining narcotic pain relievers with brain-altering psychiatric medications sets up a perfect storm for sudden death, suicide, and other physical and psychological reactions.

After viewing the movie Concussion, I noticed that although mention was made to the deceased players using medication for pain relief, as well as psychiatric medications, there was no direct reference to these medications contributing to the actual behavior of the players being discussed. Therefore, I feel strongly that anyone having potential CTE or TBI should be aware that the first black box warning on most psychiatric medications is suicide. As this book states, there are multiple integrative treatment modalities that can be utilized for what is a very physical (not psychiatric) impairment of CTE or TBI.

Concussion also neglects to explore the relationship between psychiatric medication and dangerous physical side effects. For example, there is a scene in which a football player (Webster), who is later diagnosed post-mortem with CTE, was given an injection of Haldol (also known as Haloperidol) after he visits the NFL team physician in a very agitated state (which is not uncommon with a brain injury). Soon after, Webster has a heart attack and dies.

"Haloperidol, is also commonly used, both intramuscularly and intravenously, to control agitated patients in the emergency room. In September 2007, the FDA released a warning that torsades de pointes and QT prolongation (Heart rhythm) might occur in patients receiving haloperidol, particularly when the drug is administered intravenously or at doses higher than recommended. The FDA notes that haloperidol is not approved for intravenous use". This information can be seen in the Summary and Comment of the 10/12/07 issue of Emergency Medicine titled "FDA Warning: Haloperidol Joins Droperidol" by Diane M. Birnbaumer, MD, FACEP.74

Also an article in the Journal Of Hospital Medicine in 2010; 5(4): E8-E16 (PubMed: 20394022) titled, "The FDA extended warning for intravenous haloperidol and torsades de pointes: how should institutions respond" reveals some patients experiencing sudden cardiac arrest after given IV haloperidol, as well as other potential risk factors.75

The movie suggests that the football player had CTE but died from heart failure; the injection of Haldol was never addressed.

CPSIA information can be obtained
at www.ICGtesting.com
Printed in the USA
LVOW13s2304080817
544321LV00009B/198/P

9 781937 801854